CAPTAIN CHARLES FRYATT
Courageous Mariner of the First World War

CAPTAIN CHARLES FRYATT
Courageous Mariner of the First World War

Ben Carver

AMBERLEY

First published 2016

Amberley Publishing
The Hill, Stroud
Gloucestershire, GL5 4EP

www.amberley-books.com

Copyright © Ben Carver, 2016

The right of Ben Carver to be identified as the Author
of this work has been asserted in accordance with the
Copyrights, Designs and Patents Act 1988.

All rights reserved. No part of this book may be reprinted
or reproduced or utilised in any form or by any electronic,
mechanical or other means, now known or hereafter invented,
including photocopying and recording, or in any information
storage or retrieval system, without the permission in writing
from the Publishers.

British Library Cataloguing in Publication Data.
A catalogue record for this book is available from the British Library.

ISBN 978 1 4456 5861 2 (print)
ISBN 978 1 4456 5862 9 (ebook)

Typeset in 10pt on 13pt Sabon.
Typesetting and Origination by Amberley Publishing.
Printed in the UK.

Trampled yet red is the last of the embers,
Red the last cloud of a sun that has set;
What of your sleeping though Flanders remembers,
What of your waking, if England forget?

Why should you share in the hearts that we harden,
In the shame of our nature, who see it and live?
How more than the godly the greedy can pardon,
How well and how quickly the hungry forgive.

Ah, well if the soil of the stranger had wrapped you,
While the lords that you served and the friends that you knew
Hawk in the marts of the tyrants that trapped you,
Tout in the shops of the butchers that slew.

Why should you wake for a realm that is rotten,
Stuffed with their bribes and as dead to their debts?
Sleep and forget us, as we have forgotten;
For Flanders remembers and England forgets.
              To Captain Fryatt, G. K. Chesterton 1922

Contents

	Foreword	9
	Preface	11
	Introduction	13
Chapter 1	Early Days and Baptism of Fire	14
Chapter 2	The Die is Cast	22
Chapter 3	Wartime Tributes and Memorials	30
Chapter 4	Destiny of the *Brussels*	37
Chapter 5	Buried with Honour	43
Chapter 6	Lest We Forget	60
Chapter 7	Associated Ships' Epilogue	75
Chapter 8	The Unanswered Questions	77
	Notes	79
Appendix A	The Fryatt Watches	84
Appendix B	German Destroyers that Captured the *Brussels*	88
Appendix C	Prisoners of War in Germany	89
Appendix D	Letters	93
Appendix E	Legalities and Rationale	96
Appendix F	*Captain Fryatt* Railway Locomotive	98
Appendix G	German Merchant Submarines	99
Appendix H	Funeral of Captain Fryatt at Dovercourt	101
Appendix I	Abbreviations	104
	Maps	106
	Bibliography	111
	Acknowledgements	113
	Index	115

Foreword

As a young boy growing up in Dovercourt in the early 1950s, I was only vaguely aware of my maternal grandfather, Captain Fryatt. It was the same for my brother and older cousins. What little we learnt came from the weekly Sunday pilgrimage to visit and tend 'the grave'. From these trips, I learnt that he was a ship's captain, but worked for the railways, which I remember seemed odd. I thought that he must have been important, as his grave was bigger than all the others and was set aside. I was told that he had been shot by the Germans in 1916.

No other information was forthcoming, this veil of silence having been strictly imposed by Grandmother since that fateful day when she became a widow, and the family continued to be secretive on the matter. We never really understood why. My grandmother was a very private woman but my mother Dorothy does remember being told that, if she talked about her father, the Germans would hear and come and get them.*

After Grandmother's death in 1956, the responsibility for the watches, medals, papers and other artefacts passed to my two maiden aunts, Doris and Olive. On their deaths, the family relics passed to my mother and her sister, Mabel. Only then was the next generation able to piece together the story and realise the part Grandfather had played in the Great War. Over recent years, interest has grown and it was this that led the family to give the collection to the Imperial War Museum.

Old habits die hard. My mother still does not really comprehend why people continue to be interested in her father and his exploits, although she was very pleased to see the 2014 *Railways at War* programme based around the Cavell Van. It is timely, a century after his execution, that this book has been written, bringing together most, if not all, of the facts about my grandfather, although the full extent of his role in the war may never be known.

Julian Fryatt Luckett
Northiam, East Sussex
March 2016

---

* Julian's mother Mrs Dorothy Luckett died peacefully on 8 May 2016, aged 102.

Preface

I embarked on this relatively brief account of the loss of Captain Charles Fryatt and his ship, the SS *Brussels*, with a view to meeting the one-hundredth anniversary of his execution in July 1916. A great deal has been written about the story over the years, mainly in the form of books, magazine articles and newspaper reports. There is also much to be found now on the internet, in addition to which I have been fortunate in gaining access to much documentation, mostly provided by the many contacts I have made in the course of my research.

All these sources were, and remain, in the public domain but, in the course of my research it became clear that much is still to be released. After the factual account I have, therefore included a series of rhetorical questions in Chapter 8. Except where opinions are expressed, I do not purport to confirm, deny or speculate on any of them but, if readers wish to explore any of them further, the book *Captain Fryatt – Patriot or Pirate* by Michael G. White (2005) is recommended reading.

An in-depth study of the legalities of the whole episode, including the trial, execution and their aftermath, can be found in *The History of the Great War – The Merchant Navy, Volume II* by Sir Archibald Hurd (1924). For deeper investigations, the National Archives at Kew would be worth a visit, although there is probably much more information at large, or else not yet released.

I have included a general list of acknowledgements of those who have helped me in my research, but I would like to mention here a few whose assistance has been outstanding – namely, in alphabetical order: Monte Banks, who assisted with general nautical matters and proof reading; Bob Clow, Harwich Railway & Shipping Museum, who gave me the run of his vast collection of railwayana and all things Fryatt; Harry Farthing in Melbourne, who discovered the 'replica' Fryatt watch out there and donated it to the Imperial War Museum; Geoff Hewitt MNI, maritime historian and help with research; Alan Leonard, Southampton local historian concerning the family's days there; Julian Fryatt Luckett, one of Captain Fryatt's grandsons who, *inter alia*, gave me copious information on both the family dynasty and on the histories of the Fryatt watches and their donation to the IWM, as well as extensive material and illustrations on the story as a whole, both contemporary and on subsequent events; Ray Plummer, chief archivist, Harwich Town Council, concerning copies of original documents; and Andrew West of Brisbane, Australia for leads on the Fryatt watches, the SS *Wrexham* painting and, together with Ric Adams, the film *The Murder of Captain Fryatt*.

In addition I am grateful to Ian Hook, keeper of the Essex Regiment Museum and Peter Williamson, Chairman of the Essex Regiment Museum Trustees, for their detailed research on my behalf into Captain Fryatt's brother William, who became a key player in the Fryatt story after the war. I must also thank John Villers of Finial Publishing, who worked wonders adapting and enhancing many of my own photographs. I have included a longer list of acknowledgements of those who have helped me in my research, whose input may have been less extensive but no less invaluable.

Although every effort has been made to seek copyright permission for the use of photographs, this has not always been possible, especially where origins could not be identified. Accordingly the author apologises for any inadvertent use of material without permission or acknowledgement and the necessary correction will be made at the first opportunity.

Finally I would like to thank my wife Meriel for her endless patience and assistance over all aspects of this work, in particular the illustrations, necessitated by my lack of computer skills.

No doubt many commemorations will be held during the centenary year of 2016, and I wish organisers well for their success. Meanwhile I hope readers will find this short account both helpful and interesting.

Ben Carver
March 2016

Introduction

At about 7.00 p.m. on 27 July 1916, the Germans committed one of the worst atrocities of the First World War. Captain Charles Algernon Fryatt, Master of the Great Eastern Railway ship SS *Brussels*, had been court martialled, even though a civilian, for attempting to ram an attacking German submarine and being a *franc-tireur*. Having been found guilty, he was executed almost immediately by firing squad, after a show trial lasting barely two hours, during which he was afforded no proper defence. As happened following the execution of Edith Cavell in 1915, the event caused international outrage, and led to Fryatt's body being repatriated after the war and given a ceremonial funeral.

Mercantile Marine Captain Charles Algernon Fryatt, about 1913.

Chapter 1

Early Days and Baptism of Fire

Charles Fryatt was born at 6 Marsh Lane, Southampton, on 2 December 1871, the second son and third child of Charles, noted in the 1881 census as a 'mariner', and Mary Fryatt *née* Percy. The birth was registered on 8 January 1872, and young Charles was baptised at St Mary's Church on 6 March 1873, by which time the family had moved to 72 Lower Canal Walk. The fifteen-month delay seems to have given rise to some confusion, causing the year of birth to be recorded incorrectly in some quarters as 1872.

The family eventually totalled seven, four boys alternating in age with three girls. Apart from the third son, William, about whom we learn more later, little seems to be known about Charles's siblings. The eldest was John Algernon who was born in July 1864 and died in September 1918, followed by Elizabeth Anne Jane, who was born in June 1869 and died in 1931. After Charles Algernon came Bessie Sophia, who was born in June 1875 but died in infancy aged six months, then William Percy, who was born in June 1877 and died in June 1960. Mary Caroline was born in 1879 and died in December 1983 and finally Algernon Percy was born in February 1885 and died in November 1966.

Young Charles was educated first at Holy Trinity National School in New Road (built in 1853 and closed in 1910) from around 1876 until he entered Freemantle School in Mansion Road[1] on 14 March 1882 after the family moved to nearby Queens Road[2]. He remained there until 22 October 1883, when the family moved to Harwich after his father joined the Great Eastern Railway Company (GER). Here they lived in a tied house in Adelaide Street, Parkeston. (See Map A)

Fryatt completed his education at Harwich Corporation School in King's Quay Street, now a private residence known as School House[3]. As a teenager he then joined HMS *Worcester*, the Thames Nautical Training College at Greenhithe on the north Kent coast. On leaving he served on various merchant ships, including the sailing ship SV (Sailing Vessel) *Ellenbank*, before joining the GER as an 'able seaman' (AB) on SS *Ipswich* (1,067 gross registered tons) in 1892 at the age of twenty, earning £1 5s per week, equating to about £150 in 2015.

When *Ipswich* was in dry dock in Hull, Charles met local girl Ethel Townend (born in 1878), whom he married on 2 November 1896. The couple set up home in Garland Road, Parkeston (see Map A), and started a family, which eventually comprised six girls and one boy. The first was Olive Annie (born in August 1897), followed by Ethel Victoria in December 1899; next came Doris Irene in May 1902, and then Vera Evelyn in March

Victorian entrance to Freemantle Primary School, Southampton. (Photograph by the author, courtesy of Freemantle Church of England Academy 2011)

Original school bell beyond the first window. (Photograph by the author, courtesy of Freemantle Church of England Academy 2011)

School House, Harwich 2014. (Photograph by the author, courtesy of the owner, Mrs Betty Holbrook)

Charles and Ethel Fryatt, believed to have been taken at the time of their wedding in November 1896. (Courtesy of Ray Tanner, Harwich TC Archivist)

1905. The last to be born while the family lived in Parkeston was Mabel Marjorie in June 1907, sometime after which they moved to Oakland Road in Dovercourt (see Map A) before their only son, Charles Algernon Sidney, was born in January 1911. The last was Dorothy Ada Mary in December 1913, born just down the road in Tendring.

Meanwhile Fryatt continued to rise through the ranks, being promoted to second mate in June 1900, earning £1 15s (equivalent to about £210 in 2015) per week. He rose to first mate in 1907 and, in June 1913, his first command was GER's 1,160 grt SS *Colchester* (in which his father had earlier been chief officer) and, later that year, he was appointed master of SS *Newmarket* (833 grt).

The twin-screw *Brussels* had been built in Dundee for the GER by Gourlay Brothers, and was launched on 26 March 1902. Her length was 285 feet overall; her beam 34 feet and depth 15.5 feet, 1,380 grt; her official number 109884 and her service speed about 14 knots. Powered by two reciprocating steam engines, each of three cylinders triple expansion, she was built to high standards of comfort and stability, and regularly sailed from Parkeston Quay, Harwich and later Tilbury, to various Dutch and (except during the war) Belgian ports (see Map B).

The ship's early career was uneventful, except for an unfortunate incident in April 1907 when she ran aground in fog off Harwich. She was re-floated virtually undamaged on a subsequent favourable tide.

At 11.00 p.m. on 4 August 1914, Britain declared war on Germany. The last civilian service left Harwich on 6 August, with passengers including Prince Lichnowsky, the German ambassador in London returning home. He had worked tirelessly to prevent Britain joining the war, and was so popular that not only was he afforded a special train to Harwich, but was welcomed there with a guard of honour. Thereafter Harwich was militarised and civilian services were transferred to Tilbury.

The strongly fortified city of Antwerp was able to delay capture by the Germans until well after they had overrun the rest of Belgium. On 6 October, the day the Belgian

Brussels in peacetime, with GER livery of black hull and white superstructure, yellow funnels with black boot topping and red below the waterline (LNER).

government relocated from Antwerp to Ostend, the *Brussels*, under the command of Captain Frederick Beeching, was the last GER ship to sail out of Antwerp. Following evacuation of civilians on 7 October, the city was formally surrendered to the Germans on the 10th. GER ships continued regular sailings to neutral Holland, largely in defiance of the Germans, who by then occupied the Belgian coast and considered that part of the North Sea to be their domain. Nevertheless, in this role there could be no question of any GER ships being armed, even if only for self-defence, as the Dutch refused entry of any such ships into their ports. No doubt the Germans were aware of this restriction.

On 4 February 1915 the Germans declared that, with effect from 18 February, all waters surrounding Great Britain and Ireland would be treated as a war zone, and that every Allied merchant vessel found there would be destroyed. The fate of passengers and crew appear to have been of arbitrary concern, with the official rather euphemistic addition being, 'without it always being possible to avoid danger to crews and passengers'. (See Appendix E). The declaration added that it would be impossible to avoid attacks on neutral ships in mistake for those of the enemy, such reference arising from the practice of both sides flying neutral flags as an acceptable *ruse de guerre*.

On 10 February the Admiralty issued supposedly secret instructions to all masters of merchant shipping, to be followed in the event of threat or attack by enemy submarines. The crucial passage read:

> No British merchant vessel should ever tamely surrender to a submarine, but should do her utmost to escape … If a submarine comes up close ahead of you with obvious hostile intentions, steer straight for her at your utmost speed, altering course as necessary to keep her ahead. She will probably then dive, in which case you will have ensured your safety, as she will be compelled to come up astern of you.

It should be noted that there was no specific instruction to ram, although it would be reasonable to assume that there was an implication to do so. Nevertheless the Germans already knew that if a captain surrendered his ship (assuming he was not captured), he would be in serious trouble. They had found a copy of the relevant directive when Ben Line's 3,100-ton SS *Ben Cruachan* was captured and then sunk by *U-21* in January 1915, about 15 miles north-west of Morecambe lighthouse, while carrying coal from Cardiff to Scapa Flow in Orkney to fuel the Grand Fleet.

On 3 March 1915 Captain Fryatt was in command of the 1,414-ton SS *Wrexham* (chartered to the GER by the Great Central Railway since December 1914), when she was attacked by a German U-boat. According to contemporary reports, the ship was chased for 40 miles, often exceeding her design maximum speed of 14 knots by as much as 2 knots. Eventually she reached Dutch territorial waters, unharmed except for a burnt funnel and, as well as the engine room crew being complimented on their efforts, Fryatt was awarded a gold half-hunter watch by the GER with the following inscription:

> Presented to Captain C.A.Fryatt by the Chairman and Directors of the G. E. Railway Company as a mark of their appreciation of his courage and skilful seamanship on March 2nd 1915.

Early Days and Baptism of Fire

Wrexham/GER half hunter watch. (Photograph by the author courtesy of, IWM, object no. 10292)

Alfred Jensen's 1904 painting of the *Wrexham*. She was returned to the GCR later in 1915 because she was too slow. (Courtesy and copyright of auctioneers GC Railwayana, ref. 10069)

On 28 March 1915, the 4,800-ton Elder Dempster Line passenger cargo ship *Falaba* was sunk by *U-28* between Pembrokeshire and the south-east corner of Ireland, while sailing from Liverpool to Sierra Leone with about 240 passengers and crew. Initially the steamer was ordered to stop, allowing time for evacuation, but when she started to send emergency wireless messages and fire distress rockets, the submarine fired a torpedo within ten minutes at very close range. There were still several passengers and crew on board, which resulted in 104 deaths. Coming barely ten days after the German declaration, the incident was a clear indication that they really meant business.

On the self-same day, the *Brussels*, which by now had been fitted with wireless telegraphy, sailed for Rotterdam with Captain Fryatt in command; this was Fryatt's 143rd crossing since the beginning of the war. She was steaming at full speed on a course determined by the Admiralty when, nearing the Maas lightship, Fryatt observed a large submarine 4 or 5 miles away on the starboard bow. *U-33*, under Kapitänleutnant (broadly equivalent to Lieutenant, Royal Navy) Konrad Gansser, signalled Fryatt to stop, which he ignored and, following Admiralty instructions, changed course to take his ship astern of the enemy. The submarine also changed course, but apparently to manoeuvre into a position to torpedo the *Brussels*. By now Fryatt had made the decision to ram the submarine, and, firing distress rockets to make it look as though the *Brussels* was armed, he headed for the enemy at full speed.

Just as the Admiralty instructions had suggested, the submarine immediately dived and, shortly afterwards, its periscope broke surface just a few feet from the *Brussels*' port bow. Although Fryatt felt nothing himself, one of the firemen reported feeling a bumping sensation, as if there had been some underwater impact between the two vessels. Nevertheless, the *Brussels* continued at full speed towards the safety of Dutch territorial waters, by which time she was out of danger. Fryatt made the following entry in his log:

> 1.10 p.m. Sighted submarine two points on starboard bow. I altered my course to go under his stern. He then turned round and crossed my bow from starboard to port. When he saw me starboard my helm he started to submerge and I steered straight for him. At 1.30 his periscope came up under my bows, port side, and passed astern. Although a good look out was kept I saw nothing else of him. The lat. was 51° 08' N., long. 3° 41' E.

Fryatt sent a detailed report to the GER Directors, detailing all the events involved in the incident and expanding on his log entry. The report concluded:

> I think I must have damaged him if I have not sunk him as I consider it was impossible for him to have got clear according to the position of his periscope when it came up to the surface. After it passed our bridge it came further out of the water showing a decided list, after which it disappeared. ... I must highly commend my Officers, Engineers and crew for the way my orders were carried out.

Following arrival at Rotterdam, the *Brussels* was taken into dry dock for inspection following the impact. The lateral scrapings along her bilge-keel and bottom provided conclusive evidence of contact.

The Germans were infuriated, and from that moment were determined to avenge Fryatt's audacity. He was praised in the House of Commons and presented with a vellum certificate dated 21 May by the Admiralty, together with another gold watch, this time a full hunter inscribed:

> Presented by the Lord Commissioners of the Admiralty to Chas. Algernon Fryatt Master of the S.S.'Brussels' in recognition of the example set by that vessel when attacked by a German submarine on March 28th, 1915

In addition the First Officer and Chief Engineer were presented with Commendations for their bravery at a civic ceremony by the Harwich Borough Mayor Edward Saunders.

During the summer the *Brussels* and other GER ships had further encounters with enemy submarines, while in the charge of other masters, which on one occasion included William Hartnell in the *Brussels*; under their skilled seamanship the ships always managed to escape. Meanwhile Fryatt continued with his normal duties, even, it is thought, commanding cross-channel troop and hospital ships, although no firm evidence of this has been found.

Admiralty hunter watch, face open. (Photograph by the author, courtesy of IWM, object no. EPH 10291)

Chapter 2

The Die is Cast

During the late evening of 22 June 1916, *Brussels* sailed from Rotterdam with Captain Fryatt, who had been in command since March 1915. Senior members of the crew included First Officer William Jessie Hartnell, Chief Engineer Frederick Thurlow, Second Engineer Frederick Joseph Starkey, Chief Steward Richard Davison Tovill and Chief Stewardess Mrs Alice Elwood. Among the passengers were Belgian refugees and a suspicious character speaking fluent German, but with an American accent. Cargo comprised foodstuffs, mainly a large quantity of pig meat, and mail, which included a sealed diplomatic bag containing confidential documents from the British Consul General in Rotterdam.

After steaming the few miles down the River Maas to Hook of Holland, where she loaded more mail, *Brussels* was starting for Tilbury at about 11.00 p.m. when Fryatt and Hartnell on the bridge, and probably lookouts elsewhere on the ship, observed a rocket fired from the shore. Next, about 12 miles past the Maas lightship, the officers detected a small unidentifiable vessel, whose lamp signalled the letter 'S' in Morse code (three dots or short flashes), the significance of which was never ascertained. Nevertheless the two incidents led Fryatt to believe, quite rightly, that something was afoot threatening his ship.

Immediately orders were given for all lights to be turned off, and for all passengers to remain below. Fryatt sensed that there was another ship somewhere in the darkness, which was showing no lights and following much the same course as his own. At about 12.30 a.m., Fryatt ordered his navigation lights to be switched on briefly to warn the other ship, wherever she was, of his presence and so avoid any collision. Hartnell described what happened next (see Appendix B):

> At 12.46 craft without lights were seen at a point on the starboard bow, travelling at a great speed in the opposite direction. These proved to be German destroyers of the latest type, five in all. Two came alongside on the starboard side and one on the port side, the other two following close behind. During the time the destroyers were approaching, their commanders were shouting orders to stop, asking the name of the ship and threatening to fire on us.

Fryatt knew he now had no option but to obey, so immediately arranged for his confidential papers and diplomatic mail bag to be taken to the engine room and thrown into a furnace. Shortly afterwards the Germans boarded his ship and ordered the passengers and crew into one of the destroyers, smashed the wireless equipment (operated by telegraphist Joseph Frestone) and then, after a few false starts with tempers flaring as they learned how to operate the machinery, brought the *Brussels* under the German flag into Zeebrugge at about 5.30 a.m. on 23 June.

The tide was then too low to enter the Baldwin Canal (completed 1907), so *Brussels* had to wait at the Mole for some three hours until at least half tide. The banks of the canal then thronged with servicemen determined to catch a glimpse of their catch, as she made her way along the 7 or so miles to Bruges with at least some of her crew. (Records vary as to how many of the crew returned on board for the short journey, but it is thought some were taken by road). Meanwhile, judging by the deference the mysterious passenger was shown, it was concluded he was a German agent, and not surprisingly he was immediately released.

On 28 June Fryatt and Hartnell, together with the rest of the male crew members, were taken to Ruhleben internment camp, formerly a racecourse at Spandau just west of Berlin (see Appendix C), while the five stewardesses[4] went first to Ghent, then Cologne, before finally arriving at Holzminden, south west of Hannover (see Map C).

Following the intervention of the US Ambassador, Mr James W. Gerrard, acting on behalf of the Foreign Office (the USA was then still neutral), the stewardesses were repatriated during the following November. The fates of the Belgian refugees were the subjects of various reports, but have never been uncovered with certainty.

Brussels under arrest in Bruges. Note the two stewardesses on deck. The military gent is probably General Freiherr [Baron] von Bütlar (see infra), with his dog on the gangplank[5]. (IWM, ref. 023358).

Four of *Brussels*'s officers shortly after capture. (Mrs Jill Burchell Collection)

Some of the *Brussels* crew formally seated, having recently arrived at Ruhleben. Captain Fryatt is absent from both these photographs. (Courtesy of City Archives Bruges – Fonds Zeebrugge, ref. ZB/FO/538)

From Ruhleben, Fryatt sent two letters to his wife, the first shortly after arriving when the rest of the crew also sent theirs, and the second on 1 July, which did not arrive until the 29th, by which time it was too late (see Appendix D). On 2 July Fryatt and Hartnell were returned to Bruges for imprisonment. Here, Fryatt was confined alone in a cell and subjected to intense interrogation in order to incriminate himself, Hartnell and masters of other GER ships.

Meanwhile Mr Gerrard was asked by the Foreign Office to appoint a counsel for Fryatt, to which at first the German authorities refused to reply. Eventually on 26 July, he was informed that Captain Fryatt would be tried by court-martial the following day at the Bruges Provinciaal Hof (literal meaning, 'provincial court').

Without having received any prior advice or assistance, Fryatt stood before the court at about 2.30 p.m. on 27 July. The President (*Kriegsgerichtsassessor*) was Dr Zapfel, and the accused was defended by a Major Naumann, a reserve officer, civil attorney and *Justizrat* (broadly equivalent to KC/QC), who understood little, if anything, of maritime traditions and rules of sea warfare as applied and understood by maritime nations. However, he did his best and requested a postponement, which was refused. Meanwhile, the flimsy charge brought against Fryatt was that, 'although not a member of a combatant force, [he] did make an attempt on the afternoon of March 28th 1915 to ram the German submarine *U-33* near the Maas Lightship'. Note the word 'attempt', in law a much lesser offence than actually succeeding.

Fryatt's cell in 1919. (Courtesy of City Archive Bruges – Collection Brusselle-Traen, ref. BRU001007415).

Provinciaal Hof, Bruges 2015. (Willy Vereenooghe)

It is sometimes claimed that the inscriptions on Fryatt's gold watches did him no favours at the trial. However, he was definitely not carrying either when captured, as they had been left in the safekeeping of his wife. Nevertheless, it is likely that German intelligence had cottoned on to the publicity of the presentations, and therefore the inscriptions as well. In any case it should be noted that the wording on the *Wrexham* watch presented by the GER was quite vague, with no reference to any encounter with a submarine. The inscription on the *Brussels* watch presented by the Admiralty, on the other hand, would have been much more incriminating.

'For operational reasons', Gansser did not attend the trial. Having left with *U-33* for the Mediterranean in August 1915, and not handing over command until September 1916, *prima facie* there is no reason for him to have been in Belgium, or even Germany, at the time. There is, however, some evidence that Gansser and *U-33* were in Wilhelmshaven in July 1916, so the ship and crew may have returned for some reason, such as for leave or a refit, which is supported by two members of the crew, Leutnant Wieder and Matrose (meaning 'Seaman') Richter, giving evidence. Such surmise is further supported by the submarine's records showing she inflicted no shipping losses between the end of April and the middle of September in 1916. In any event, Gansser's absence would probably have been a matter of convenience on account of the potential embarrassment over allowing *U-33* to be struck by the *Brussels*, although not surprisingly he made no mention of any contact in *U-33*'s log.

Court-martial room in the Provinciaal Hof. (Source unknown)

William Hartnell later recalled that, 'when he [Fryatt] rose to his feet to speak for himself, there was not a German present who could face him'. After brief deliberations, the court found Captain Fryatt guilty and at 4.30 p.m. sentenced him to death; the sentence was confirmed by Admiral Ludwig von Schröder, Commandant of the Marinekorps Flandern, at 5.00 p.m. Had Fryatt cited the Admiralty order of February 1915, it is likely that the court would not have convicted him. He remained silent, however, although it would be reasonable to assume that by then the Germans would have become aware of the order.

At 7.00 p.m. Fryatt was taken, still in civilian clothes, to the Hof van Aurora (sometimes known as the Beluik der Gefusilleerden, literally translated as 'Courtyard of the Executed', as it was where Belgian 'traitors' were shot by the Germans), part of the barracks close to the canal at Kruispoort on the eastern side of the city, and named after the Roman goddess of the dawn. Here he was executed by firing squad in the presence of Freiherr von Bütlar, of whom little is known except that he probably held a fairly senior military rank; a German Lutheran naval chaplain called Köhne, who subsequently wrote to Mrs Fryatt (see Appendix D), and two Belgian councillors. The senior of these two was Victor Van Hoestenberghe, Alderman of the city and later to become Burgomaster of Bruges, while the name of the other was Descheppen.

The following notice of the execution was published in German, Flemish and French, signed by von Schröder and dated 27 July 1916:

The English captain of the Mercantile Marine, Charles Fryatt of Southampton [sic], though he did not belong to the armed forces of the enemy, attempted on March 28th

Half-crown coin with ribbon, reputedly given to a nun in Bruges by Captain Fryatt before his execution. (Photograph by the author, courtesy of IWM, object no. EPH 200)

1915 to destroy a German submarine by running it down. This is the reason why he has been condemned to death by judgement this day of the War Council of the Marine Corps [sic] and has been executed. A perverse action has thus received its punishment, tardy but just.

The Captain's body was placed in a makeshift coffin and buried in the Central Cemetery at Assebroek, an eastern suburb of Bruges where executed Belgians were also buried, with a simple black cross erected over the grave. Personal effects, comprising his wallet, gold cufflinks, a purse with two gold half sovereigns and a small travelling set of dominoes, were subsequently returned to Mrs Fryatt from Ruhleben.

It has never been fully established whether the Kaiser ordered a stay of execution, which was possibly mislaid or even conveniently ignored, nor even whether he was consulted at all. However, on 9 August 1919, *The Times* reported that a telegram from Berlin ordering postponement of the execution arrived in Bruges half an hour after it had been carried out.

Covering a visit by Mrs Dorothy Luckett and her family to the execution site in 1993, the *De Klant van West-Viaanderen* (a local paper known as *KW*) reported that Van Hoestenberghe was obliged by Admiral von Schröder to witness the execution. He had remembered that the German High Command was not at all happy with the verdict and that, hardly an hour after the execution, a cable was sent from Berlin to change the death penalty to imprisonment.

An article in the *New York Times* of 24 October 1918 included the following report sent from Bruges a few days earlier, as the Germans were preparing to leave the city ahead of the Armistice:

> **Bruges 21st October.** German rule in Bruges was marked by a combination of cruelty and corruption without parallel since the days of Spanish tyranny in Flanders. By Schröder's orders hundreds of persons have been shot after the travesty of a trial on the scantiest evidence.

The report continued with a comment from Dr Zapfel:

> The British will want my head in payment for Fryatt's life, but it is Schröder alone who is responsible. I simply obeyed his orders, which insisted absolutely on the death penalty.

Readers can draw their own conclusions as to the verdict of what amounted to a brief show trial, and the indecent haste with which that verdict was executed.

Chapter 3

Wartime Tributes and Memorials

Outrage, both at home and abroad, followed. In the House of Commons, Prime Minister Herbert Asquith issued a statement on 31 July saying that Fryatt had been 'murdered' by the Germans and that those responsible would be brought to justice, although this never happened[6]. Lord Claud Hamilton MP, Chairman of the GER, denounced the atrocity as 'sheer, brutal murder', while newspapers throughout the world, not only in the UK, its allies and the Empire, but also in neutral countries such as the USA, Holland and even Switzerland, reported in similar vein. As would be expected there was a volley of self-justification and propaganda across the German press.

King George V, who it should be remembered was first cousin to the Kaiser, wrote to Mrs Fryatt expressing abhorrence over the outrage (see Appendix D). On Sunday 6 August, there was a large protest demonstration by the British Workers League in Trafalgar Square, at which a statement from Mrs Fryatt was read out:

> I feel deeply this sympathy extended by my fellow countrymen in my sad bereavement. It is a great consolation to think that the British Empire Union are determined that the perpetrators of this foul crime on my dear husband should be punished.

The Imperial Merchant Service Guild telegraphed Mrs Fryatt:

> Words cannot convey to you the disgust we feel at the most despicable crime yet perpetrated by Germany. The whole of the merchant service join in sympathy for you and in mourning the loss of our member, Captain Fryatt, whose name as a hero and martyr of the profession to which he belonged will be handed down to generations of seafarers.

Mrs Fryatt was awarded a pension of £250 per annum (equivalent to about £24,000 in 2015) by the Great Eastern Railway, supplemented by a further £100 p.a. by the Government. Fryatt's insurers, what was then known as the Provident Clerks & General Mutual Life Assurance Association, paid the £300 to which she was entitled immediately, without bothering with the usual formalities, and the Royal Merchant Seamen's Orphanage, now known as the Royal Merchant Navy School Foundation, offered to educate two of her seven children, whose ages then ranged between two and a half and

Mrs Fryatt, shortly after the execution. (Adapted by Author, Bob Clow Collection)

eighteen years. Probate was granted on Fryatt's estate on 20 September in the sum of £1,073 16s 7d (around £100,000 at 2015 values) bequeathed to his widow.

Memorials abounded, both during and after the war. Some of the wartime dedications were quite informal, such as the RA gunners on the Western Front, who were so moved by the incident that they bombarded the Germans with shells inscribed 'TO CAPTAIN FRYATT'S MURDERERS' on them.

Gunners on the Western Front in France, with 15-inch shells about to be delivered to the enemy, August 1918. (From the albums of General Sir Richard Harte Butler. Crown Copyright IWM, subject ref.1900-09, image ref Q. 942).

Later in 1916, publishers Hodder & Stoughton rushed out an anonymous propaganda booklet entitled *The Murder of Captain Fryatt* costing 2d, the front cover of which was enlarged to become a wartime poster. The booklet was later distributed worldwide in several different languages[7].

In March 1917 the London & North Western Railway's new steam locomotive No. 154 was named *Captain Fryatt* (see Appendix F). Initially the Dutch branch of the League of Neutral States presented the GER with a memorial, located in the main booking hall at Liverpool Street station. It was unveiled on 27 July 1917, the first anniversary of Fryatt's death, and comprises a bronze portrait prepared by the Dutch sculptor H. T. H. Golberdinge, whose signature can just be discerned on Fryatt's right shoulder. The roundel is mounted on a marble tablet, on which is inscribed:

> To the Memory of Captain Charles Fryatt July 27th 1916. From the Neutral Admirers of His Brave Conduct and Heroic Death. The Netherlands Section of the League of Neutral States July 27th 1917.

Captain Fryatt was posthumously awarded the Order of Leopold, the Belgian Maritime Cross and the British War Medal, all of which were presented to the IWM by his descendants in 2011[8].

Front cover of 1916 booklet. Note the initials 'F. G.' under the Captain's elbow, which was the signature of the celebrated poster artist F. G. Cooper (Photograph by the author, courtesy of Bob Clow)

The family outside their home in Oakland Road shortly after the execution. The little girl on her mother's lap is Captain Fryatt's youngest child Dorothy, who was born in December 1913 and died in May 2016.

Fryatt memorial at Liverpool Street station. (Photograph by the author, courtesy of Network Rail)

Order of Leopold. (Photograph by the author, courtesy of IWM, object number OMD 4245)

Belgian Maritime Cross. (Photograph by the author, courtesy of IWM, OMD 4246)

British War Medal (Photograph by the author, courtesy of IWM, OMD 4244)

In 1917 a quay at Centreport, Wellington (originally Port Nicholson), New Zealand, which had been established between 1904 and 1916, was named after Captain Fryatt. Some of the original Fryatt Quay structure became landlocked following reclamation in the late 1960s of the area seaward of the wharf, for the establishment of the Thorndon Container Terminal. Reclamation was followed by the construction of Shed 39 for cargo use adjoining the original quay; in 2005 it was converted to a two-storey office building, which still exists.

Also in 1917 a propaganda film entitled *The Murder of Captain Fryatt* was made in Australia[9] (see Appendix A). The blurb on the publicity poster said it was

> the first and only cinema production of this apotheosis of the calculated ferocity of the Hun. Every detail of the awful atrocity is presented with absolute fidelity and historic fact. Stirring incident upon incident unfolds the deeply designed crime against humanity, culminating in the cold blooded murder of one of the noblest of the Empire's Mercantile Marine heroes.

The film, however, appears to be far removed from the truth, made apparent by the *Adelaide Advertiser* of 25 June 1917, in its column ironically headed 'Amusements':

> ... there is the additional attraction of a film dealing with the shooting of Captain Fryatt by the Germans. The picture introduces Captain Fryatt at the Admiralty offices, and shows the presentation of the watch as a recognition of his services in sinking a German submarine. Next the Captain's homecoming is illustrated and he is depicted as the

happy father of a large family. A spy intrudes and gains the confidence of the seaman. There follows the sailing of the *Brussels*, the appearance of a German submarine and the disembarkation of the captured passengers and crew in Germany. In prison Captain Fryatt meets an old Belgian who reveals to him the identity of the spy by telling him the sorrowful tale of his own experiences. When Fryatt is led out to his doom, the spy arrives to mock him, but the Captain fells him to the ground then turns to face the bullets of the soldiery.

So much for absolute fidelity and historic fact!

Shed 39, seaward facing, about 2010. The original line of the quay ran through the car park in the foreground. (Neville Hyde)

Chapter 4

Destiny of the *Brussels*

Renamed *Brugge* by the Germans in 1916, the *Brussels* was used initially as a submarine depot ship at Zeebrugge but, before the Germans evacuated the port in October 1918, she was sunk as a blockship off the head of the Mole. When the Allies liberated Belgium soon afterwards, the harbour was found to be in chaos, with all kinds of sunken vessels, including the *Brussels*, completely obstructing its use.

Having been in the service of the Germans and retaken in Belgian waters, *Brussels* was considered a Belgian prize and therefore owned by the Belgian government. Accordingly the Belgians are likely to have asked the Admiralty to salvage the *Brussels*, as they were the most experienced salvors worldwide, especially in the removal of harbour wrecks. Furthermore the Belgians probably had to pay for her removal, as she was not a British vessel on charter to the British government under War Risk (the main criterion for Admiralty salvage operations), unless some other deal was struck.

Postcard of the sunken *Brussels*. (Alan Leonard Collection)

The Admiralty salvage expert Cdr G. J. Wheeler RN was charged with clearing the harbour and returning it to proper use as quickly as possible. He was assisted by Lt R. Brooks RNVR who had special responsibility for the *Brussels*, by then 18 feet into the mud that almost filled her. By early June 1919, Wheeler had surveyed her sufficiently to learn that she had not been torpedoed in the Zeebrugge raid as originally thought[10], but internally mined. There were two holes of about 5 feet in diameter on the starboard side, one of which was near the bilge keel, and there was another hole of similar size in the corresponding position low on the port side. In addition, the brass ports had all been removed for the German war effort, so carpenters made covers for fitting over the portholes prior to pumping out.

Next, Wheeler decided that the *Brussels* would have to be lifted bodily, a deadweight of nearly 4,000 tons including the hull full of mud. The tide at Zeebrugge rises an average of 18 feet, sufficient for the lifting vessels to raise the steamer to the top of the hole left in the mud. Four of the lifting craft could raise 5,000 tons, an ample margin and, by pumping out their submerged tanks as the tide rose, another 4 feet of lift could be gained, sufficient to carry the steamer over the lip of the hole and out of the congested harbour.

Every day brought difficulties, be it the weather, delays with progress on other vessels and even labour problems. Eventually, on 3 July the salvage vessel *Linton* managed to secure the first 9-inch cable under the *Brussels* but, as it became so badly chafed by broken plates, it had to be abandoned. On the next day a 6-inch guide wire broke but, by 16 July, five lifting wires had been secured, but not without first having to remove the bridge, which was obstructing the operation; by 26 July all sixteen lifting wires were in position.

Brussels being raised in Zeebrugge harbour in 1919. (LNER)

Meanwhile three further lifting vessels that had been deployed on other wrecks were made ready for the *Brussels*. By close of play on Saturday 2 August, all was ready for lifting on the following Monday 4 August, which coincidentally was the fifth anniversary of Britain's declaration of war. All went to plan with the actual lifting and, apart from an initial hitch of an unslipped anchor wire on one of the salvage vessels, the collection of craft moved slowly as a unit for 2 miles eastwards, until the wreck touched the bottom at a depth of 37 feet off Heyst. On the next day she was moved inshore until she lay in 30 feet of water at high tide. When the tide had ebbed on 6 August, the *Brussels* lay in only 8 feet of water. She was in a bad state, covered in barnacles and weed, having been submerged for nearly a year.

Following salvage, the ship was patched up, refloated and towed to Antwerp. On 26 April 1920, as an act of international courtesy, she was handed over with ceremony to the British Government by the Belgians, with the provision that any monies raised by her sale should be put towards a lasting memorial to Captain Fryatt. The Belgians were represented by their Minister of Marine M. Poulet and the British by their ambassador Sir

Brussels off Heyst, after being raised and moved along the coast. (*Illustrated London News*, copyright John Weedy)

Francis de Villiers. It was reported that, on behalf of HM King Albert, Poulet gave to Sir Francis the Belgian Maritime Cross posthumously awarded to Fryatt.

Having been escorted down the Scheldt River by the light cruiser HMS *Dragon* (4,850 tons), *Brussels* left for the Tyne on 17 May under tow of the Admiralty tug *St Clement* commanded by Capt. C. H. Richardson DSC, assisted by the Belgian tug *President de Leeuw*. In command of the *Brussels* was Capt. F. H. Bryant DSC and she was once again flying the Union Flag. She arrived at the mouth of the Tyne at about 9.30 p.m. on 20 May after a rough and delayed crossing and, at 5.30 the following morning, against a slight haze and a picturesque rising sun, she started to move upstream. The *Shields Daily Gazette* reported:

> Hardly a ripple troubled the water and the ship lay quietly about a mile from the piers, a curious object in these days of trim craft with her foremast gone, her after funnel out of line and her rails and bulwarks battered, and in places gone entirely. ... By 7.30 the procession of vessels had passed within the piers, and coming slowly onward the Blue Ensign was dipped at Lloyds hailing station. There were numerous people on the piers, and vessels in the river sounded their sirens in the usual lusty manner ... On the ferry landings, large numbers of people had collected, and workmen in the yards downed tools for a few minutes as the famous ship went slowly past.

By 9.00 a.m. the *Brussels* was safely moored at Jarrow Quay corner, alongside Ellerman Wilson Line's SS *Eskimo* (3,325 tons). The Mayor of South Shields, Ald. Robertson, and his party were received on the ship by Capt. Bryant. After an exchange of speeches, the Mayor hosted a civic reception.

Eventually *Brussels* was sold for £2,700 to J. Gale & Co. (Gale Shipping Co. Ltd of Preston) and taken to Leith to be converted to a cattle boat at Henry Robb's Shipyard. In this guise, her gross tonnage was reduced to 1,090 (see Appendix J) and she could carry 600 head of cattle and 1,000 sheep. She then ran under the flag of the Dublin & Lancashire Steam Ship Co. for service between Preston and Dublin, far removed from her once-proud existence as a luxury passenger and mail steamer. She first arrived at Preston to much acclaim, including that of the Mayor, Alderman T. Parkinson and the town clerk, Mr A. Howarth, on 5 September 1921. The *Preston Guardian* (as it was then known, later *Gazette*) reporting on 17 September:

> The arrival of the Brussels in its new home naturally attracted an unusual amount of local attention. It was a great disappointment to many hundreds that she missed the tide on Sunday afternoon, but those who were able to make a second visit after her arrival on Monday were fully compensated for their trouble.

Preston is an artificial harbour, dug from marshland in 1892, about 9 miles upstream of the River Ribble. In 1921 the port was up-and-coming and was pleased to obtain the business, albeit anything as humble as the cattle trade. *Brussels*'s first departure in her new role was on 7 September under Captain D. I. Ronayne. On 29 October, the *Guardian* reported that, although she had begun her association with the port of Preston over a

Brussels first arriving at Preston on 5 September 1921. (LNER)

month previously, she was already filling an important niche in the Anglo-Irish cattle trade, and bidding fair to make the town a distributing centre for the north.

On 22 March 1922 the Guild Mayor of Preston, Henry Astley Bell, unveiled a memorial plaque, presented by the Captain Charles Fryatt Memorial Fund[11] on the bridge, on which the wording reads:

> Captain Charles Fryatt when gallantly endeavouring to save this ship and the lives on board from capture during the Great War was himself taken prisoner and subsequently shot. His name is honoured in the history of the British nation and his deeds have added lustre to the records of the British Merchant Service.

In August 1922 the D&LSS Co. was taken over by the British & Irish Steam Packet Co., which in 1923 changed the name to *Lady Brussels*, in keeping with the names of various other ships in the fleet prefixed *Lady*[12][13]. Under this guise, she continued to ply between Dublin and Preston, but eventually her age, damage and time under water took their toll. On 19 April 1929 she arrived in Preston for the last time and, early the following month, she started her final voyage, to the Clyde for breaking up by ship-breakers Smith & Co. at Port Glasgow, having been replaced by a new cattle boat *Lady Meath* (see Chapter 7).

Unveiling the plaque on the bridge of the *Brussels* by the Guild Mayor of Preston (Lancashire Lantern Archive, Image ref. 4280, Lancashire County Council and Preston City Council)

Chapter 5

Buried with Honour

Shortly after the Armistice, the GER magazine for December 1918 made the following report:

> The grave in Bruges Cemetery has been visited by the British Minister at The Hague, Sir Walter Townley. It was marked by a black wooden cross and is beside the graves of six devoted Belgians who were also shot without justice; upon it the sexton had placed an anchor of small cactus plants. The Captain's name is now painted white on the black cross* and Lady Susan Townley placed a wreath of immortelles tied with British colours upon the grave.

*The inscription reads, 'Here lies Captain Fryat [sic] Master of the SS Brussels of glorious memory RIP'.

Captain Fryatt's grave, Bruges, shortly before disinterment. (Copyright Dover Museum ref. D37814)

Captain Fryatt's body was exhumed at about 8.30 p.m. on Friday 4 July 1919, with his younger brother William[14] and William Hartnell present to identify the body; also in attendance was Mr A. C. Pain, a director of the GER and their agent in Antwerp. The old coffin with body still inside was transferred to a new, more fitting coffin, which was escorted to a temporary chapel of rest at the Provinciaal Hof in Bruges; here it was placed on a catafalque draped with the Union Flag and guarded by Belgian soldiers[15].

On Sunday 6 July the coffin left the Provinciaal Hof, borne by eight Forbes-tartan-kilted sergeants of the 10th (Scottish) Battalion of the King's (Liverpool Regiment), more commonly known as the Liverpool Scottish Regiment. The detail was commanded by Lt A. McF. Cram, who was on attachment from the Liverpool Scottish Queen's Own Cameron Highlanders (both Territorial units). At the bottom of the steps outside, on which the Kaiser had once been photographed with the much-hated Admiral von Schröder, the coffin was carefully transferred to an ornate hearse drawn by a matched pair of black horses and flanked by the pall-bearers, who in turn were flanked by a guard of an equal number of Belgian soldiers, with the chief mourner William Fryatt behind. The procession started at 12.20 p.m. and comprised more Belgian soldiers, Boy Scouts, a band, military commanders and government, provincial and city dignitaries, among whom was the British Ambassador to Brussels, Sir Francis de Villiers. The route to the station thronged with mourners, with flags at half-mast at every step.

At the station the coffin was loaded onto the special train by the pall-bearers, to the band playing La Brabançonne, the Belgian National Anthem. The VIPs boarded, the guard presented arms and, with the band still playing, the train started at 12.50 p.m.; it arrived at the architecturally splendid Middenstatie station, Antwerp, at 3.40 p.m. after covering approximately 55 miles. Here the coffin was received by a guard of honour comprising 100 men of the Liverpool Scottish and twenty-five of the Leicestershire Regiment (the 'Tigers'), and carried down the main hall of the station by the pall-bearers. It was then loaded onto a Belgian Artillery gun carriage drawn by six horses, to the strains of Chopin's Funeral March played by the band of the 15th Regiment of the Line.

Captain Fryatt's coffin in the Proviciaal Hof with Belgian guard, before starting its journey home. (Courtesy of City Archives Bruges, ref. BRU001001348 – Collection Brusselle-Traen)

The procession from the Middenstatie was led by the Pipe and Military band of the Liverpool Scottish, and now comprised a British contingent led by the band, three English mounted policemen, a detachment of French Chasseurs Alpins and a US army detachment in field dress. The gun carriage followed, flanked by the pall-bearers, and on the coffin were two large wreaths, one from the city of Antwerp and the other from Their Majesties King Albert and Queen Elisabeth of the Belgians, with others from the city of Brussels and the GER. Following the gun carriage came the official mourners, again comprising William Fryatt, Sir Francis de Villiers and various civil and military dignitaries. An estimated 10,000 people lined the streets, with Belgian flags at half-mast and street lamps draped, with over 500 dignitaries and officials, mainly with maritime connections and many with their ladies.

The procession arrived at Quay 21 at the harbour, where the 1,000-ton 'Moon' class destroyer HMS *Orpheus* (1916-1921) under Commander M. B. Birkett DSO was waiting. Level with the bows of the ship was a large dais on the quayside, which accommodated no fewer than five people – three civilian and two service clergy (in contrast to not a single minister being present at Bruges). The gun carriage halted by the dais, while the procession marched to its allotted places. There followed a short service ending with the sailors' hymn, 'Eternal Father Strong To Save', after which Belgian General Hannoteau pinned to the coffin the Knight's Cross of the Order of Leopold.

Now, for the last time, the eight Liverpool Scottish pall-bearers took the coffin onto their shoulders and carried it to the foot of the gangway, which was lined on one side by the original guard of honour, which presented arms as the coffin approached.

The Last Post was sounded by the Chasseurs Alpins as the coffin started its precarious ascent of the rather awkward gangway and, following its successful negotiation, it was piped aboard the destroyer and lowered onto the waiting catafalque on the quarter deck. Escorted officially by two French and two Belgian torpedo boats and, unofficially, by a flotilla of small craft, all with flags and ensigns at half mast, *Orpheus* slipped her moorings at about 5.30 p.m. and made her way down the River Scheldt to the open sea, arriving at Ostend Roads at 9.45 p.m.[16].

Procession passing Manfield's branch, Antwerp, 6 July 1919.

Procession elsewhere in Antwerp, with Cathedral in background. (Courtesy of Liverpool Scottish Museum Trust)

Before the start of the service on the quay at Antwerp, with dais in background waiting to be occupied by the clergy (Courtesy of LSMT, ref. 0864)

Coffin ascending gangplank (Courtesy of LSMT, ref. 0863)

Coffin guarded aboard HMS *Orpheus* approaching Dover. (Courtesy of Laurie Manton, the Graveyard Detective)

At Ostend *Orpheus* weighed anchor at 12.05 p.m. the following day, 7 July, and later that afternoon she was escorted into Dover harbour by the destroyers *Taurus* and *Teazer* (both of similar size to *Orpheus*), while all vessels present lowered their ensigns to half-mast. Once a naval vessel had brought the VIPs ashore, the coffin was transferred by the dockyard launch *Adder* to the naval pier, where it was received by six Royal Navy Reserve ratings, who carried it to a waiting gun carriage.

The procession through Dover was led by the chief constable of Dover Borough Police, D. H. Fox (Kent Police in those days comprised a number of smaller forces), followed by the band of the Chatham Division of the Royal Marines. An RM guard with reversed arms preceded the gun carriage, which was drawn by a full team of RNR ratings and flanked by pall-bearers representing the South Eastern & Chatham Railway and others. Immediately behind were William Fryatt and Mrs Claxton (wife of the Master of the GER SS *St Dennis,* which was then in Dover acting as hospital ship), who represented Captain Fryatt's widow.

The rest of the procession comprised officers and seamen of the Royal Navy and Mercantile Marine ships in port at the time (the latter had not by then been renamed the Merchant Navy), representatives of the GER and SE&CR, Scouts, the Royal Air Force and the infantry garrison at Dover. At the rear came the General Officer Commanding Dover and Rear Admiral Commanding the Dover Patrol (Sir Roger Keyes, of Zeebrugge raid fame), together with their respective staffs.

The route to Dover Marine station was lined with dense crowds and, on arrival, the RNR pall-bearers carried the coffin into the waiting railway van, PMV [Parcels and Miscellaneous Vehicle] No. 132[17], which was draped in purple. Here, the coffin remained overnight and, on Tuesday 8 July, the van was attached to the 7.35 a.m. train for London. At Chatham it was detached and joined a special train, carrying an RN detachment and

Orpheus entering Dover Harbour. (IWM, copyright ref. SP2820)

Procession through Dover. (Copyright Dover Museum ref. D37969)

PMV No. 132 at the Kent & East Sussex Railway before restoration. (Courtesy of Lewis Brockway)

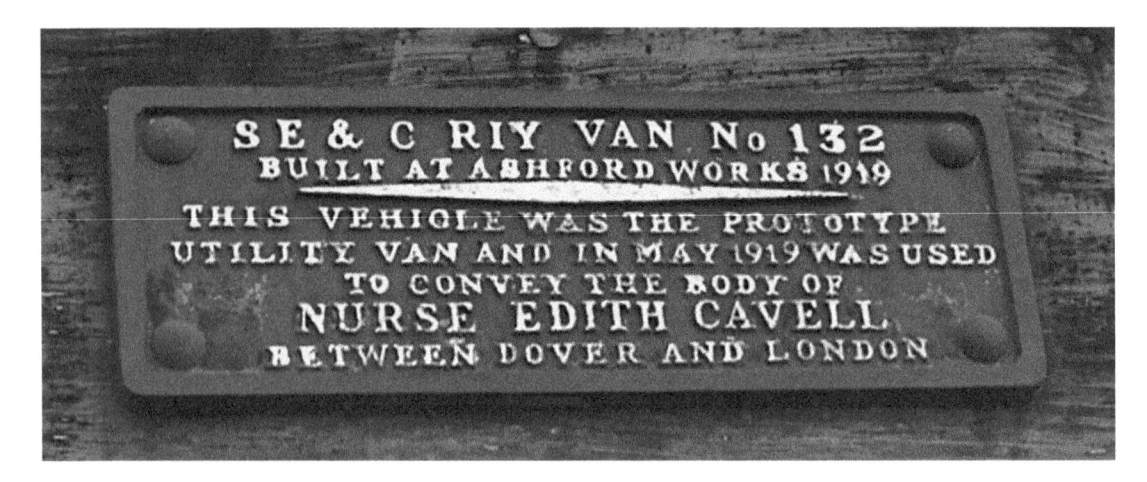

Builders' plate on vehicle. (Courtesy of Lewis Brockway)

PMV No. 132 following restoration in 2010. (Courtesy of Lewis Brockway)

the RM Chatham band, which arrived at Charing Cross station at 11.00 a.m. From here, it was borne on a gun carriage to Trafalgar Square, down to and along the Embankment, up to Ludgate Hill and then to St Paul's Cathedral for the Memorial Service.

Procession leaving Charing Cross station for St Paul's Cathedral. (*Illustrated London News*, copyright John Weedy)

The service was attended by members of the royal family and hundreds of merchant seamen or their widows. The government was represented by members of the Admiralty, the Board of Trade, the Cabinet and the War Office, while the pall-bearers were Captains Barren, Goodney, Lawrence and Stiff, fellow Masters of Great Eastern Railway ships. Music was provided by the GER Musical Society, supplemented by Royal Marine drummers, and the service was conducted by the Right Reverend Arthur Winnington-Ingram, Bishop of London.

An unidentified local Hampshire newspaper (probably the *Hampshire Chronicle*) reported the event thus:

> A wonderfully impressive scene was witnessed in London when the body of Captain Charles Fryatt was conveyed in procession through the streets of the City for the memorial funeral service at St Paul's Cathedral ... when for the first time London saw in a state ceremonial officers and men of that great service, our Mercantile Marine.

Crowds lined the route of the coffin to Liverpool Street station, from where the funeral train was hauled by GER D15 Class locomotive No. 1849[18] to Dovercourt, near Harwich, where it arrived at 4.00 p.m. and was then taken by gun carriage for reburial

Coffin entering St Paul's Cathedral, borne by bluejackets. (*Illustrated London News*, copyright John Weedy)

Chief mourners entering St Paul's. Mr and Mrs William Fryatt leading, with Captain William Hartnell on their left. (*Illustrated London News*, copyright John Weedy)

Buried with Honour 53

Coffin leaving St Paul's. (*Illustrated London News*, copyright John Weedy)

Front cover of Order of Service. (*Illustrated London News*, copyright John Weedy)

St. Paul's Cathedral.

Funeral of
Captain Charles Algernon Fryatt,
Master of the
Great Eastern Railway Company's
S.S. "Brussels,"
who was Murdered by the Germans,
July 27th, 1916, at Bruges, Belgium.

July 8th, 1919.

at All Saints Church. The processional route from the station was up Kingsway, along Marine Parade, into Fronks Road, then left into Main Road for the short distance to the church (see Map A).

The procession included the Diocesan Bishop John Ditchford of Chelmsford, Suffragan Bishop Robert Whitcombe of Colchester and Suffragan Bishop James Inskip of Barking[19], although it is uncertain where they joined it; GER representatives, numerous naval and military personnel; the Shotley Band; the massed Bands of the Cambridge, March and Stratford Railways; and local civic dignitaries and organisations, with the route lined by thousands of local people paying their respects. The procession culminated at the grave at the northern end of the churchyard, where the Bishop of Chelmsford led the service during which the body was laid to rest (see Appendix H).

On 18 June 1920, a memorial over Captain Fryatt's grave was unveiled. The GER magazine of August 1920 described the memorial as being simple yet dignified in Portland stone, the work of Messrs Farmer and Hindley of Westminster Bridge Road [London SE]. The top was surmounted by the badge of the Mercantile Marine, while underneath the inscription there was a wreath of laurel leaves with the words 'Pro Patria' in the centre. The inscription reads:

> In memory of Captain Charles Algernon Fryatt, Master of the Great Eastern Steamship, Brussels, Illegally executed by the Germans at Bruges on the 27th July, 1916.
> Erected by the Company as an expression of their admiration of his gallantry.

Funeral train locomotive, suitably draped, with 'F'-inscribed wreath. (Adapted by the author, courtesy of Bob Clow)

Funeral procession on Marine Parade led by the three bishops, opposite the corner with Lee Road. (Courtesy of the Harwich Society)

View taken from the same spot as the picture above in 2014. (Author)

Procession approaching All Saints Church, Upper Dovercourt. (Courtesy Harwich Society)

Graveside tribute. (Courtesy Harwich Society)

Buried with Honour

> **Upper Dovercourt Churchyard.**
>
> Funeral of
> Captain Charles Algernon Fryatt,
> Master of the
> Great Eastern Railway Company's
> S.S. "Brussels,"
> who was Murdered by the Germans,
> July 27th, 1916, at Bruges, Belgium.
>
> July 8th, 1919.

Front cover of Order of Service. (Bob Clow Collection)

The Fryatt Memorial shortly after unveiling, with a view of Parkeston Quay beyond. (Courtesy Harwich Society)

Fryatt Memorial in 2014, showing a subsequent development blocking view beyond. (Author)

Inscription on the memorial, 2014. (Author)

Before the unveiling, moving speeches were made by Lord Claud Hamilton (not only chairman of the GER but also High Steward of the Borough of Harwich) and Rear Admiral G. R. Mansell, CBE, MVO (later Vice Admiral Sir George Robert Mansell, KCVO, CBE, MVO), representing the Corporation of Trinity House[20]. After the unveiling by His Lordship, a brief service of dedication was conducted by the Rev. T. Grey Collier and concluded with the national anthem.

The Times correspondent reporting on the event concluded with these moving words:

> Now he was in a quiet place where sailor men have lived and loved and died since there were ships. A place welded by time and tradition to the sea and holding the bones of not a few of those who knew the ocean in their day and helped to keep it free.

Chapter 6

Lest We Forget

There are numerous memorials in many forms dedicated to Captain Fryatt, which appeared worldwide after the war. The ultimate local dedication was the provision of a new hospital in Dovercourt. Local residents and organisations had wanted a hospital for some years and fundraising had started in 1913 but, with the outbreak of war in 1914, the matter had been shelved. After the war, the project resurfaced under the guidance of the Mayor of Harwich Edward Saunders, who played an important part as benefactor and fundraiser.

By December 1921 sufficient funds had been raised to purchase a suitable building for £4,000 (about £167,000 in 2015), a residence known as *Rosebank*, which had been built by the Mayor Edward Saunders in 1911. By now it was occupied by Commander Coysh, who was the Marine Superintendent at Parkeston and also choirmaster at St Paul's Church, Parkeston. Meanwhile, £2,100 of the money raised by the sale of the *Brussels* had been donated to the cause and it cost a further £8,000 to adapt and equip the hospital, with annual running costs put at £1,200.

The hospital was officially opened with much ceremony by Lord Claud Hamilton, in April 1922. The *Harwich & Dovercourt Standard* reported:

> … on receiving a silver key from Master Charles Fryatt, the only son of the late Captain Fryatt, His Lordship declared the hospital open 'to the glory of God, for the alleviation of the suffering and for the help of the sick, and in memory of the late Captain Fryatt'.

The hospital was named the Fryatt Memorial Hospital and a ward was named after him. Charles Fryatt had been aged five at the time of his father's death, and eleven at the opening ceremony.

The hospital continued to evolve and improve, with new facilities being introduced. During the Second World War, it continued to serve local needs, although beds were set aside for emergency war cases, all greatly assisted by the local Red Cross Voluntary Aid Detachment. On a few occasions there were admissions for air-raid injuries, with a major incident being ten survivors of the 7,900-ton Royal Netherlands Steamship Co. (Koninklijke Nederlandsche Stoomboot Maatschappij) liner *Simon Bolivar*, which sank after hitting a mine in November 1939.

Front cover of the hospital opening ceremony programme. (Courtesy Bob Clow)

Hospital about 1924. (Celia Strachan collection)

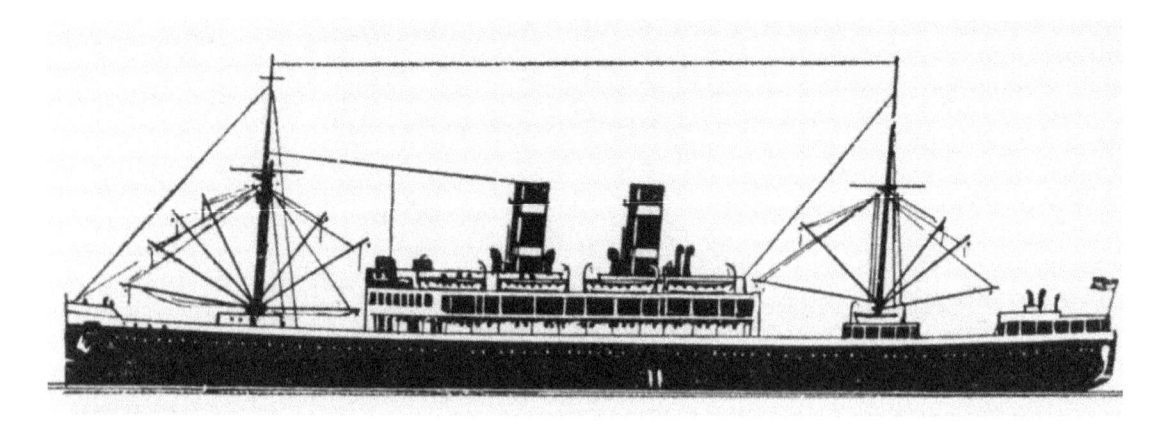

Profile of 7,900-ton *Simon Bolivar*, built for the Royal Netherlands Steamship Co. in 1927.

With the introduction of the NHS in 1948, the hospital was handed over to the Ministry of Health. The loss of its independence was mourned by many but, on the positive side, the town no longer had to raise funds and maintain a hospital service whose costs by then were rising sharply due largely to advances in medical treatment.

By the late twentieth century, it had been decided to build a new hospital, which was completed by the end of the 2005 and opened in 2006. Apart from the hospital itself, the complex comprises the Mayflower Medical Centre, a nearby pharmacy and adequate free parking facilities. It is now known as the Fryatt Hospital and Mayflower Medical Centre, Harwich.

The plaque appears to have been installed in the original hospital in about 1982, when there was some disagreement over the proposed wording. Doctors did not like the phrase 'killed by the Germans' in view of some of the patients of that nationality coming ashore at Harwich. They preferred the word 'enemy', but eventually a compromise appears to have been reached with the wording 'executed by the Germans'.

In the official history *The Merchant Navy*, Sir Archibald Hurd wrote,

> Captain Fryatt's innocence is alike attested by British history, by British laws and by British privileges at sea. He upheld a right which is vital to those who go down to the sea, and defend it with constancy, loyalty and unflinching courage.

At home there is the Captain Fryatt public house in Garland Road, Parkeston, which was built in the 1880s and first named the Garland Hotel; its name was changed as recently as the 1970s (see Map A).

A short distance away in Dovercourt is Fryatt Avenue, also on Map A.

In Belgium Kapitein Fryatt Straat runs along the west side of the old locks in Zeebrugge, which the Royal Navy rammed in April 1918. In 1942 the Germans, again in occupation of Belgium, changed the name to Azores Straat but, after the Second World War had ended, the name Fryatt was reinstated. Further afield there are other locations incorporating the name Fryatt in both England and Belgium, with others elsewhere in Europe, in the USA, Australia (where feelings about Fryatt's death were particularly

Lest We Forget

Fryatt Memorial hospital, Dovercourt, 2014. (Author)

CAPTAIN C.A. FRYATT

THIS HOSPITAL WAS PROVIDED AS A MEMORIAL TO CAPTAIN CHARLES ALGERNON FRYATT, MASTER OF THE GREAT EASTERN RAILWAY STEAMSHIP, "BRUSSELS", EXECUTED BY THE GERMANS AT BRUGES ON 27TH JULY, 1916, AFTER ATTEMPTING TO RAM A GERMAN SUBMARINE.

ERECTED BY THE HARWICH SOCIETY

Plaque inside main entrance. (Author)

Captain Fryatt public house, 2014. (Author)

Pub sign on the extreme left of the above photograph. (Author)

Fryatt Avenue street sign, looking south, 2014. (Author)

strong), New Zealand (see Chapter 3), South Africa and even Mauritius. In 1921 two mountains in Jasper National Park in Alberta, Canada, were named in Fryatt's honour, namely Mount Fryatt (11,027 feet) and Brussels Peak (10,371 feet) after the ship.

The inscription on the Fryatt Memorial erected in the Hof van Aurora in Bruges 1922 reads:

> Capt. Fryatt Charles of Southampton [sic] died for his King and Country on July 27th 1916 at the age of 44.
> Erected by the English Convent, Bruges

Twelve other similar columns commemorate Belgian civilians also shot by the Germans during the war. The site is the place of execution and is now a memorial garden (not a cemetery) where the bullet holes can still be seen in the wall, known as the Mur des Fusilles.

To complement the memorial, a plate originally taken from the hull of the *Brussels* was positioned on the wall near the entrance to the site. It is inscribed in both English and Flemish, and includes a sketch of the ship:

> The SS Brussels belonging to the Great Eastern Railway Company & commanded by Captain Fryatt was captured by the Germans on the 22nd/23rd June 1916 near the

The Fryatt Memorial, Bruges, identified in Hof van Aurora in Chapter 2.

Detail of the inscription (Erf-goed.be collection, courtesy of Willy Vereenooghe)

William Hartnell (left) and William Fryatt at the unveiling ceremony of the Fryatt Memorial, Bruges on 19 July 1922. (Topfoto ref. EU010565)

King Albert at the unveiling of the Fryatt Memorial, 19 July 1922. (Courtesy of City Archive Bruges, ref. BRU001000315 – Collection Brusselle-Traen)

Schouwen Bank. This plate belonging to the SS *Brussels* has been offered by the British War Office.

In 1922 Fryatt's 1917 memorial at Liverpool Street station was incorporated into the GER War Memorial, which was originally located in the main booking hall where, on 22 June, it was unveiled by Field Marshal Sir Henry Wilson, MP for North Down. It was then dedicated by the Right Reverend Bertram Pollock, Bishop of Norwich, in the presence of Lord Claud Hamilton, several GER directors and employees, as well as a large audience. The inscription reads:

> To the glory of God and in grateful memory of those members of the Great Eastern Railway Company who, in response to their call of their King and Country sacrificed their lives during the Great War

In August 1923, the Fryatt Memorial received a belated consecration by the Bishop of Barking, then was formally unveiled again by Col. W. J. Galloway, a GER director. The composite memorial, which also includes Sir Henry Wilson, who was assassinated by Irish Republican Army (IRA) gunmen on his way home after the 1922 unveiling, is now located just inside the gallery entrance to the station, following completion of the station modernisation in 1991.

Plate from the hull of *Brussels* in Hof van Aurora. The inscription SPQB below stands for *Senatus Populus Que Brugensis*, translated as 'The Government and People of Bruges'. See the transcription above. (Alan Leonard collection)

In November 2007 the Fryatt Memorial was featured in a Channel 4 programme about war memorials in general. Some of the passing rail travellers were asked what it meant to them but most knew little or nothing about it, and were not particularly interested.

Battlefield tourism in France and Belgium became big business in the 1920s, not least the German defences along the coast of the latter. In his 2013 article in the Dutch-language magazine *Der Grote Rede* (which describes itself as an information magazine on the coast and sea of the Flemish region), entitled 'Battlefield Tourism on the Coast after WW1', Alex Deseyne wrote, 'Zeebrugge even featured Chalet Fryatt, a café-restaurant, speciality raisin bread and waffles, where objects such as the late Capt. Fryatt's chair from SS *Brussels* and other famous souvenirs were on display'.

Around 1930 a tulip, *Tulipa* 'Captain Fryatt', was bred at Haarlem in Holland. It is described as 'a garnet red lily flowered variety, gracefully reflexed and flowering early-mid May'. It has not been produced commercially since the end of the twentieth century, so its availability is now very limited. There are, however, examples in the Cambridge University Botanic Gardens.

The war memorial at Liverpool Street station, containing the names of 1,108 GER employees killed in the war. The Fryatt memorial is in the centre below the GER names, with Sir Henry Wilson's to the right. (Photograph by the author, courtesy of Network Rail)

In July 2006 there were memorials in both Harwich and Bruges to mark the ninetieth anniversary of Captain Fryatt's execution. The exhibition in the Guildhall, Harwich, was entitled *Captain Fryatt Remembered*, where there were displays on the Fryatt family both before and after the event, First World War submarine warfare, the capture of the *Brussels,* the trial and execution, the repatriation, and the ceremonial reburial of his body after the war. There were artefacts on view and a commemoration service was held at All Saints Church, Dovercourt, during the evening of 27 July, the date of the execution.

On 14 September 1936 *The Times* reported that a memorial tablet had been unveiled in the English church in Bruges on the previous day, by Mr Henry Tom, British Consul-General in Antwerp. The ceremony was attended by various British and Belgian civic dignitaries and Royal Navy officers, and among the subscribers were several British individuals and organisations, including the LNER and the Imperial Merchant Service Guild. The church was closed in about 1984 and became a concert hall, following which the tablet was transferred to the Provinciaal Hof. In January 2007 a bronze replica was presented to Fryatt's old school, Freemantle Primary (now known as Freemantle Church of England Community Academy), which surprisingly was the first time that he had been honoured in the city of his birth.

All Saints Church, Upper Dovercourt, 2014. (Author)

HARWICH TOWN COUNCIL

EXHIBITION

CAPTAIN FRYATT REMEMBERED

JULY 2006

The 90th Anniversary of his Execution

The Guildhall, Harwich, Essex

Front cover of programme of the 2006 commemorations in Harwich. (Harwich Town Council)

> **LIST OF EXHIBITS**
>
> **Introduction**
>
> **The Fryatt Family – the Early Years**
>
> **World War I & the Submarine Threat**
>
> **Capture of ss 'Brussels'**
>
> **Trial of Captain Fryatt**
>
> **Execution**
>
> **Homecoming and Funeral Services**
>
> **Fryatt Family – afterwards**
>
> **Why?**
>
> **Memorabilia**

List of exhibits taken from programme. (Harwich Town Council)

In the presence of several members of the Fryatt family and various Belgian representatives, the plaque was unveiled by the captain's great niece, Mrs Dot Stewart, having been presented to school representatives in Bruges a few days beforehand. The inscription on the plaque reads:

> To the memory of Charles Fryatt Master of the SS Brussels condemned to death and shot in this city July 27th 1916 by the enemy in occupation. His body was conveyed to England in HMS Orpheus July 6th 1919 and laid to rest in Dovercourt. The Mur des Fusilles near the St [sic] Kruispoort marks the scene of his execution.

The *Southampton Daily Echo* of 27 January 2007 reported on the events of the previous day that 'It was, incredibly, the first time Southampton had officially honoured its home-grown hero'. Mrs Stewart was quoted as saying, 'I am thrilled that at last Southampton has honoured him ... I hope the children will feel inspired. I feel grateful to the school and honoured that at last he is being recognised here'.

In 2014, arrangements were made by some of Captain Fryatt's descendants to have his name added to one of the Southampton Cenotaph memorial glass panels. The name was not included originally, probably because the family moved from Southampton over thirty years before the outbreak of war, and this being his place of birth had been overlooked. The name was unveiled at that year's Remembrance commemorations, in the presence of several of those descendants.

At the time of writing, plans were in hand for a plaque commemorating Captain Fryatt to be installed in the Holyrood Merchant Navy memorial, Southampton, in time for the centenary of his execution in 2016. The structure of the memorial is the preserved ruin of twelfth-century Holyrood church, destroyed by Second World War bombing.

Southampton Cenotaph in 2015, showing the inscribed First World War Memorial glass panels, just discernible to the right. (Author)

A row of the glass panels on the south side of the Cenotaph reserved for First World War names. Due to lack of space, however, Captain Fryatt's name can be found on one of the panels on the north side. (Author).

The ruins of Holy Rood Church, home of the Holyrood Merchant Navy Memorial, Southampton, 2015. The MN badge can be seen above the gateway. (Author)

Chapter 7

Associated Ships' Epilogue

The *Brussels* was replaced by the appropriately named SS *Bruges*, rather larger at 2,950 tons and faster at 21 knots, which had been built by John Brown and entered service in January 1921. Within two years, ownership, along with the whole of the GER, had been transferred to the London & North Eastern Railway following railway grouping at midnight 1922/23. She was eventually sunk by air attack off Le Havre on 11 June 1940 during the evacuation of France.

U-33 had been commissioned in September 1914, with Gansser as her first captain until March 1917. She had a surface displacement of 685 tons, a surface speed of 16-17 knots and a crew of thirty-five. She remained in the North Sea and eastern Atlantic until August 1915, following which she sailed for the Austro-Hungarian naval base at Cattaro in the Adriatic, and later Constantinople (known as Istanbul since 1930). She finally left for Kiel in October 1918, surrendered at Harwich in January 1919 and later that year was broken up at Blyth in Northumberland.

U-33's war can best be described as destructive, having sunk eighty-five ships of about 194,500 tons, with a ship toll of thirty-five British, sixteen Italian, eleven French, nine Russian, six Greek (neutral), four Norwegian (neutral but favouring the Allies), two Japanese, one Spanish (neutral) and one US, with damage to eight more including three British and one Belgian. Her most infamous kill, with Gansser still in command, was the French-owned Russian hospital ship *Portugal* (5,550 tons) in March 1916, off Rizch in Turkey at the eastern end of the Black Sea. Her largest was the 11,000 ton

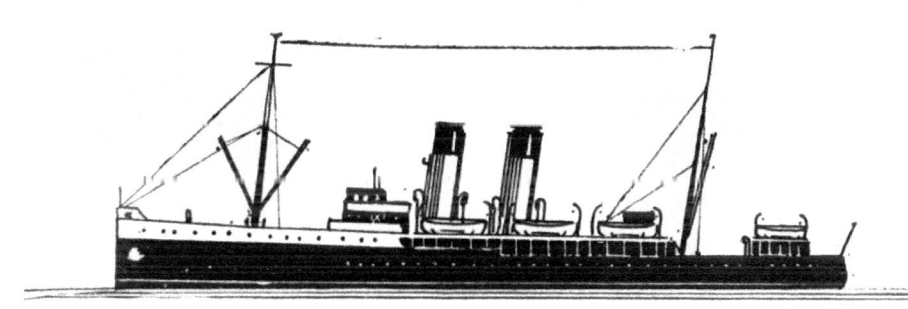

Profile of 2,950-ton SS *Bruges*, which entered service in 1921.

troopship *Cameronia* east of Malta in April 1917, this time under Gansser's successor Kapitänleutnant Gustav Sieß shortly after he had assumed command. Perhaps the former deed was the reason why Gansser was on the list of suspected war criminals, although the Russians at the time would probably have been too pre-occupied with their own internal problems to press for any conviction[6].

Ironically there was another *U-33* involved in the Second World War, a type VIIA U-boat of 500 tons, commissioned in 1936. After initial successes sinking Allied shipping totalling over 19,000 tons, mainly west of Scotland and also minelaying in the Bristol Channel, her final mission was to lay mines in the Clyde where she was sunk in February 1940 by the minesweeper HMS *Gleaner* (displacement: standard 815 tons, fully loaded 1,370 tons). At least one Enigma coding machine wheel, which should have been ditched, was captured. Seventeen survivors were taken prisoner, and the twenty-five that perished were buried initially in Greenock Cemetery, but later reinterred in the German section of Cannock Chase Military Cemetery in Staffordshire.

The SS **Wrexham** had been built in Middlesborough in 1902 as the Russian *Nord II* for the Helsinki run (Finland was then under Russian rule). She was purchased by the Great Central Railway in March 1905 to commemorate the year in which the GCR reached Wrexham by virtue of acquiring the Wrexham, Mold and Connah's Quay Railway. Despite escaping from the German submarine in March 1915, she was considered too slow, certainly slower than the *Brussels*, for the wartime conditions and duly returned to the GCR. She was requisitioned by the Admiralty in October 1916 for use as an ammunition carrier, ran aground and was wrecked at Chavanga as she entered the Gulf of Archangel (*Arkhangelsk*) in northern Russia in June 1918. The city was being occupied by Allied forces and White Russians as a base for their unsuccessful campaign against the Bolsheviks.

Lady Brussels was replaced on the Preston–Dublin cattle run by **Lady Meath**. Built at Ardrossan and slightly larger at 1,598 tons, she entered service in April 1929. In 1938 her name was changed to **Meath**[20], and she was eventually sunk by a German magnetic mine off Holyhead in August 1940.

1,600-ton *Lady Meath*, which replaced Lady Brussels in 1929.

Chapter 8

The Unanswered Questions

So concludes the factual account of the story. However, there is much left to surmise and speculation, which is beyond the scope of this narrative, largely because many German records, no doubt meticulously maintained at the time in consistency with their *modus operandi*, conveniently disappeared before the Allies could get hold of them after the war. Here, then, are a few questions, for which readers can draw their own conclusions through various sources available.

Why were Parkeston Quay and all GER ships requisitioned by the government, which announced the fact in Holland in the specialist shipping newspaper, *Lloyd Anversois*, in probability mainly for the benefit of the Germans?

Government-requisitioned ships were not RN ships as, to be so, they would have to be commissioned, and probably commanded by an RN, RNR or RNVR officer. As GER ships were not commissioned, they were neither privately operated nor in RN service. Most civilian commercial ships used for the war effort were chartered, but remained under private ownership or management. The status of the *Brussels* and other GER ships, therefore, was rather an anomaly.

Holland was a hotbed of British military intelligence, certainly with links with the Belgian espionage system, for which many inhabitants paid with their lives. Holland was the only country with a neutral frontier with Belgium, which was not only an active battleground for the opposing armies but also provided the routes of German troop movements to and from France. At one stage the Germans made an official complaint to the Dutch government, and there were even reports that the Germans considered invading Holland to suppress the spying. Did Fryatt have links with these activities which were, and to an extent still are, supported by rumours that he was even working for MI6?

Were the secret documents being carried by the *Brussels* really destroyed before she was captured? It was claimed that a courier carrying intelligence documents from the British Embassy in The Hague to London was captured, which may have accounted for the demise of at least some of the Belgians commemorated with Fryatt in the Hof van Aurora.

Similarly when the SS *Colchester* was captured in September 1916, bags of secret reports were thrown overboard but unfortunately they floated and some were recovered by the Germans before they could sink. Both the *Brussels* and the *Colchester* were captured as a result of carefully planned operations by the Kriegsmarine. Was there more to Fryatt's anti-U-boat activities, which particularly interested the Germans?

When Fryatt was first captured, he was treated quite congenially by the Germans. However, why did their attitude towards him harden once the contents of the *Brussels* documents had become known, if indeed they were captured rather than destroyed? Was there supposedly no reference to the captured documents at the trial, to ensure that it was not divulged that the Germans knew so much about the Allied spying?

Despite Admiralty instructions to do so, why is there no record of either the *Wrexham* or *Brussels* making distress calls when under threat of attack, with Fryatt in command on both occasions.

Did GER ships, under the guise of government control, carry lucrative drugs, in particular opium, to Holland, obtained through British interests in the Far East arising from the Opium Wars with China in the nineteenth century? This may sound far-fetched, but if the market was there ... ?

Did the Germans know that Fryatt was in command of the *Brussels*, both during the incident with *U-33* and when she was captured? Due to their intelligence network in Rotterdam, and to some extent in Harwich and even Tilbury, it is quite likely they did on both occasions. Even if they did not realise it at the time, the subsequent publicity, when both sides were desperate to promote heroes, would have ensured they learned retrospectively that Fryatt was in command when both the *Wrexham* and the *Brussels* evaded submarine attack, so paving the way for his capture[21].

Why did the Germans wait nearly fifteen months before capturing Fryatt and the *Brussels*, while having unlimited opportunities and resources to do so? Was there a hidden agenda, other than the visit of the *Deutschland* to America (see Appendix G)?

Apart from trying to get him to incriminate himself and his colleagues, why was Fryatt interrogated so intensively for over three weeks, when the Germans had much of the information they needed, especially following Gansser's written submission?

If not already released, will crucial information ever be available, now that the one-hundredth anniversary of Fryatt's execution has arrived?

Notes

1. Freemantle School still exists on the same site, albeit now with the rather grander title of Freemantle Church of England Community Academy. Most of the original buildings were redeveloped in the 1970s, and there were further refurbishments and extensions in 2011. The school bell still hangs outside one of the original buildings.
2. The house was No. 33 and called Cypress Cottage. Some sources record it as Cyprus Cottage but, in view of the Victorian vogue of naming houses after flowers and trees, the former is more likely. In 1903 the road was renamed Queenstown Road, to eliminate duplication of such street names.
3. The school was established in 1794 but closed in 1909 when Harwich High School was opened. It was later used as an annex to Harwich Further Education Centre, and in 1981 the building was restored from a derelict condition to a dwelling, which is now called 'School House'.
4. The full complement of stewardesses comprised Mrs Alice Elwood (head), Mrs Catherine Stalker, Miss Kate Bobby, Miss Edith Smith and Miss Clara Elwood. It is not known whether Alice and Clara Elwood were related, although it seems likely.
5. The photograph was taken by a photographer from Bruges, engaged especially by the Marinekorps. The story goes that having been ordered to destroy the plate after the print had been taken, he hid it among some rubbish for later retrieval.
6. On 2 April 1919 a German international war commission known as the Schücking Commission reconfirmed Fryatt's sentence, 'The execution by shooting of Captain Charles Fryatt, which was given by the Court Martial Bruges, due to the sentence of the court-martial proceedings on 27th July 1916, contains no violation of international law. The Commission apologises most vividly [sic] for the hurry in which the judgement was enforced'.

    The commission's ruling was not unanimous. Two members of the legal review panel dissented because, in their opinion, Fryatt's sentence had been a severe infringement of international law.

    Under Article 228 of the Treaty of Versailles, signed in June 1919, a list of 900 alleged war criminals was presented to the Germans by the Allies in February 1920, for standing trial at the Leipzig Supreme Court between May and July following. The list included Admiral von Schröder, Gansser and even the Kaiser but, in the event, nobody involved with the Fryatt case was charged, probably due to the convenient disappearance of the German documentary evidence. In any case the Dutch refused to hand over the Kaiser in exile in Holland, claiming it would violate their wartime neutral status.

7. The author approached Hodder and Stoughton concerning the availability of any copies still in existence, but was informed that all their records were destroyed by a direct hit during the Second World War London Blitz. The author is aware of only a small number of original copies, although others probably still exist. In 2011, however, the booklet was reproduced in the United States with the suffix (1916) added to the title. In addition the author is now shown fictitiously as Charles Algernon, being the forenames of his subject (see under Bibliography).

8. The Order of Leopold was instituted by King Leopold I in July 1832. It is the highest order of Belgium and awarded only by royal decree for extreme bravery in combat or for meritorious service of immense benefit to the Belgian nation. The three divisions are Military, Maritime (in practice rarely awarded and only in respect of their Mercantile Marine as the Belgian navy is covered by the Military Division) and the Civil Division. Each division has five classes; Grand Cross, Grand Officer, Commander, Officer and Knight. Captain Fryatt posthumously became a Knight (Chevalier) of the Maritime Division of the Order of Leopold.

    The two further medals comprise the Belgian Maritime Cross and the British War Medal. However, it is surprising that Captain Fryatt did not receive the Mercantile Marine War Medal, to which he would normally have been entitled in conjunction with the BWM.

    However, he was not entitled to the Victory Medal, which could only be awarded to merchant seamen who transferred to or from the armed services during the hostilities.

9. The film was directed by John F. Gavin and released on 26 February 1917, with a run time of forty-four minutes. The stars were Harrington Reynolds as Captain Fryatt and Olive Proctor as Mrs Fryatt, with Percy Walshe, Jack Gavin, Vera Bruce and Augustus Neville. Despite extensive enquiries no trace of the film could be found, although it may still exist somewhere; the National Film and Sound Archive of Australia in Canberra, however, holds a variety of still photographs.

10. The Zeebrugge Raid on St George's Day 23 April 1918 was a surprise attack to destroy the base and block the canal, both of which the Germans were using to great effect against Allied North Sea and English Channel shipping. It was regarded as a suicidal mission, but by speed and daring it succeeded in its aims, albeit with significant casualties. Different accounts have been cited about the sinking of the *Brussels*. An early conclusion was that she had been sunk by the Royal Navy during the raid but, although it is possible she was damaged, she was not sunk. The *GER Magazine* of December 1918 said she had been torpedoed by the Dover Patrol during the previous October, but inspection prior to refloating discounted the use of torpedoes.

    The most likely explanation is that the *Brussels* was sunk by the Germans by internal mining, to both act as a blockship and to cause maximum disruption for the Allies to clear once the port had been liberated.

11. The Captain Charles Fryatt Memorial Fund was founded in 1916 by the Imperial Merchant Service Guild of which Fryatt was a member. The fund provides for the relief of shipmasters and officers of the Merchant Navy and their dependants in cases of sickness, unemployment or other distress, and is now administered by the Nautilus Welfare Fund at Wallasey.

    Despite extensive research in both the UK and Belgium, it has not been possible to ascertain what happened to the plaque when *Lady Brussels* was broken up. Perhaps it went the way of the ship.
12. The catalyst for the transfer was the new service's unwelcome competition to the well-established B&ISPCo.'s service to Liverpool. It was alleged that the Dublin Port Authority purposely hindered the new service by, in particular, allocating a tidally restricted berth when more suitable berths were available. An inquiry by Dail Eireann upheld this view but David did not beat Goliath on this occasion, and by August 1922 – only eleven months after coming into service – *Brussels* transferred to the new ownership.
13. At that time B&I had a system of naming their Irish Sea ships after Irish counties, prefixed by 'Lady'. Clearly the company wanted their *Brussels* to have a *Lady* prefix, but did not want to lose the historic association of the name, hence the rather odd choice. B&I eventually gave up their *Lady* prefixes to existing names in 1938.
14. William Percy Fryatt (1877-1960) joined the army in 1904 and served mainly with the Essex Regiment. He fought with the 2nd Battalion at the Retreat from Mons, where he was wounded in September 1914, probably at the First Battle of the Aisne. He was invalided home and joined the 3rd Battalion and in February 1917 he was transferred to the Scottish Rifles (Cameronians), with whom he served at home for the rest of the war. He was discharged from the Army in May 1919, having been awarded the 1914 Star, sometimes less correctly known as the Mons Star.
15. It is not known for certain which unit provided the escort and guard, but is likely to have been either the Liverpool Scottish or Leicestershire Regiment. Both were part of the British garrison at Antwerp, and provided detachments for the repatriation ceremonies.
16. It is uncertain why Antwerp was chosen as the port of departure, as it otherwise played no part in the Fryatt story. Zeebrugge or Bruges were both totally relevant and favoured by the Belgians, with Bruges being accessible by a destroyer along the canal, as it had been by the *Brussels* three years earlier. However, the British preferred Antwerp, which probably afforded better publicity than, say, the Mole at Zeebrugge, and won the day.
17. Two months previously the same vehicle had carried home the body of Nurse Edith Cavell, executed by the Germans in October 1915 for helping allied troops escape from Belgium. Its third such use was to return the body of the Unknown Warrior for burial with full military honours in Westminster Abbey on 11 November 1920, the second anniversary of the Armistice.

    The vehicle, known to railwaymen as the Cavell Van, remained in main-line service until 1946, when it was relegated to secondary duties. It was restored at Derby at a cost of £35,000, and dedicated at the Kent & East Sussex Railway on 10 November 2010, to mark the ninetieth anniversary of the van's journey from Dover carrying the

Unknown Warrior. It is presently used at the K&ESR as an interpretation feature about Edith Cavell, Captain Fryatt and the Unknown Warrior, with a further panel about the van's place of birth – Ashford Railway Works.

18. Some sources state incorrectly that the relevant locomotive was the D14 Class prototype No. 1900 *Claud Hamilton,* named after the GER Chairman. No other 'Clauds' were named but for some reason consecutive locomotives initially numbered backwards from 1900. None was preserved after the demise of the class and its successors upto 1960, although a new-build 16/2 class 'Super Claud', to be named *Phoenix* and numbered 8783, is at a very early stage with the Claud Hamilton Locomotive Group, which is accommodated at the Whitwell & Reepham Railway at the preserved W&R station in Norfolk.

19. It is not known why the Bishop of Barking was present, although he was known to have officiated at several GER memorial functions after the war. Perhaps he was chaplain to the GER but, most likely, apart from the Diocesan Bishop of Chelmsford, he was simply the most senior churchman in the area of Stratford, GER's main depot extensively redeveloped for the 2012 Olympics. A further, albeit tenuous, link is that

CLAUD HAMILTON nameplate with descriptive panel at Wakes Colne, Essex 2014. Both were previously displayed at the former GER head office in Bishopsgate, London EC2, near Liverpool Street station, which eventually became the offices of Eastern Region BR. These premises were redeveloped in the 1990s. (Photograph taken by the author, courtesy of East Anglian Railway Museum)

his brother, Thomas Walker Hobart Inskip, was Admiralty representative on the War Crimes Committee. Persistent enquiries of the erstwhile Bishop of Barking, however, elicited no reply.

20. The main concerns of Trinity House are the safety of shipping and welfare of seafarers, brought about mainly by overseeing lighthouses and lightships, as well as harbour and river pilotage. It was granted a Royal Charter by King Henry VIII in 1514, although its origins can be traced back to Alfred the Great; nevertheless, it is unlikely that there was much continuity till the Tudor period. There remains an active base in Harwich.

21. In August 1931, the *Ottawa Citizen* reviewed a recently published book entitled *In the Enemy's Country* by Joseph Crozier, a wartime director of French espionage. He claimed that his network in Rotterdam had uncovered details of a German plan to capture the *Brussels* and arrest Captain Fryatt, and that he so informed the Admiralty. The encounter duly materialised at the time and place expected.

Appendix A

The Fryatt Watches

There were in fact three watches, two of which have already been described. Both these watches remained with Mrs Fryatt after the Captain's death and when she died in September 1956 they became the property of her two unmarried daughters, Olive and Doris, along with the medals, papers and other artefacts. After they both died, in May 1989 and April 1994 respectively, the family archive, which included the watch presented by the Admiralty, passed to the Fryatts' youngest daughter (and youngest child) Dorothy Luckett. The watch presented by the GER went to the fifth daughter, Mabel, who by then had become Mrs Oxenham.

The origin of the third watch is uncertain, but it appears to be a copy of the watch presented to Captain Fryatt by the Admiralty, inscribed with the same wording. It was discovered in Australia by Mr Harry Farthing in a tin chocolate box of assorted items, when sorting through his mother's belongings after her death in 1999. He paid little attention to the watch at the time, assuming it had belonged to his grandfather. In June 2010, Mr Farthing's grandson Tom, then aged nine, opened the back of the watch while playing with it, and the inscription was revealed.

The Farthing family is not related to the Fryatts in any way, so it is a mystery how the watch came into the possession of Mr Farthing's mother. However, he then set about locating the descendants of Captain Fryatt, with the intention of returning the watch to them. He contacted three Fryatts in Australia and three in the UK, all of whom were related to Captain Fryatt, but none was a direct descendant.

After painstaking research and enquiries, Mr Farthing eventually managed to trace one of Captain Fryatt's grandsons, Peter Luckett, who then put him in touch with his mother, Mrs Dorothy Luckett, Captain Fryatt's youngest and sole surviving daughter, and his brother, Julian; it then transpired that they had in their possession the original watch presented by the Admiralty. They had no idea how the replica came to be in Australia, and various possibilities have been considered, but in the author's view the most likely explanation is that it was made for use in the propaganda film *The Murder of Captain Fryatt*, made in Australia in 1917(9), which contains a scene in which he is presented with a watch.

Mr Farthing decided to present his watch to the Imperial War Museum, which in turn prompted the Fryatt family to donate the original watch, along with the other watch presented to Captain Fryatt by the GER, to the Museum. On 10 May 2011, there was a large gathering of Fryatt descendants at the IWM, as well as Harry Farthing and his

Still photograph from the film *The Murder of Captain Fryatt*. Although the watch is still in its case, it is no doubt more apparent elsewhere in the film. (From the National Film & Sound Archive of Australia, ref. 764258).

wife Helen. Mrs Luckett was unable to attend to present the Admiralty watch, so was represented by her sons Peter and Julian. The GER watch was presented by granddaughter, Mrs Tessa Goddard, daughter of Mrs Mabel Oxenham, who had died in 1996. In July 2011, the author was privileged to photograph all three watches at the IWM.

The wooden stand made by Harry Farthing is a copy of a stand that was quite common at the time of fob watches. It is catalogued by the IWM as having a round base made of ironwood with a depression in the centre. There is an arch made of mulga with a brass hook suspended from the centre (ironwood is the wood of *Acacia estrophiolata*, while mulga is from the *Acacia aneura*. They are both slow-growing trees from the Arid Zone of Australia, and the timbers are very hard and favourites of woodturners). On the underside of the base is a brass plaque inscribed:

For
FRYATT WATCH
Mulga and Ironwood
Melbourne
Australia
Harry Farthing
10th May 2011

Harry Farthing told the author that he found tracking down the Fryatt descendants and following the history of Captain Fryatt one of the most exciting and fulfilling experiences of his life.

Family gathering at the IWM in May 2011 for the presentation of the Fryatt watches to the Museum – all left to right.

Harry Farthing and Julian Luckett, Captain Fryatt's grandson. (Judith Luckett)

Julian Luckett, Judith Luckett and Tessa Goddard (Captain Fryatt's granddaughter). (Harry Farthing)

Harry Farthing, Paul Goddard (Tessa's husband), Simon Luckett (Peter Luckett's son) and Peter Luckett (Julian's brother). (Harry Farthing)

'Film' watch and stand. (Photograph by the author, courtesy of IWM, object no. EPH 10290)

Appendix B

German Destroyers that Captured the *Brussels*

Reports on the number of destroyers involved vary between two and five. There are firm records that there were only two, but the author considers the most likely figure is four. In the heat of the moment Hartnell could well have been confused, as it seems that five warships to capture one relatively small unarmed passenger vessel would have been rather excessive. Nevertheless, some smaller vessels, not identified at the time, may have been somewhere at the scene.

The two definites were 'grosse torpedoboote' (equivalent to destroyers) *G101* and *G102,* commanded by Kapitänleutnants Schulte and Barendorf respectively. 312 feet long and carrying a crew of around 100, the destroyers displaced 1,136 tons standard (1,734 tons fully loaded), were capable of 33 knots and were armed with four 105-mm guns and four 450-mm torpedo tubes; in addition they could carry twenty-four mines.

Both had been built by the Krupp Arms Works in the Germaniawerft shipyard, Kiel (hence the 'G' prefix) as part of a batch of four (*G101-4*) intended for the Argentine navy. Still under construction at the beginning of the war, they were all immediately requisitioned for the German navy. *G101* was to be named *Santago* and was launched on 12 August 1914, while *G102* was to be named *San Luis* and launched on 16 September. Both had fought at the Battle of Jutland, 31 May to 1 June 1916.

The other two destroyers were probably *G103*, launched 14 November 1914 and to be called *Santa Fé*, and *G104,* launched 28 November 1914 and to be called *Tacuman*, both having also fought at Jutland. If there was a fifth vessel, it was unlikely to have been as large as the others.

The German High Seas Fleet, *Kaiser Hochsee Flotte* (literally translated as 'Imperial Fleet of the High Seas'), surrendered on 21 November 1918 and was escorted into Scapa Flow. All four destroyers were scuttled by their crews, together with much of the rest of the German surface fleet (nearly all the U-boats went into Harwich) on 21 June 1919, the day the Treaty of Versailles came into effect. *G101* was raised and scrapped in 1926, while *G102* was beached and assigned to the US Navy, which sank her as a bombing target in July 1920. *G103* was raised in September 1925, but sank in a gale while being towed to the breakers' yard, while *G104* was raised and scrapped in April 1926.

Appendix C

Prisoners of War in Germany

Account by AB George Annis Calver, then aged about seventy-five, of the capture of the *Brussels*, the trial and his life as a prisoner of war in Germany. The text is taken from the *Harwich & Dovercourt Standard* of 15 July 1966, marking the fiftieth anniversary of Fryatt's execution, and republished courtesy of the *Harwich & Manningtree Standard* (to be read in conjunction with Map C).

… There is a lighthouse at Ymuiden [§] and when we came out of the Hook it seemed to be on fire. It was one big blaze. I didn't take any notice of it, but they reckoned it was a signal to the German destroyers that we were coming. Two hours run from the Hook we doused our steaming lights and just had two side lights on. All at once we saw four destroyers. We thought they were ours on patrol, but they weren't.

They cut across our bows and went well to the north east. The next thing we knew was that they were all round us. The commander in charge asked the ship's name and what we had aboard, also where we were bound. We were running into [sic] Tilbury then. He told us to stop. 'One touch on your wireless and I will sink you', he said. We were also carrying dispatches. Captain Fryatt was in a fix, so he ordered someone to take the box of dispatches out of his cabin to the stokehold and burn them, and this was done. The fires had only just been filled up and there wasn't very much room.

They transferred us from the *Brussels* to the destroyers. They transferred us again from the destroyers, and put us aboard the *Brussels*, and escorted us up to Bruges. We stopped for about three days, and then we were put on a train for a town near Berlin, where there was a racecourse[¶]. There we were kept as civil Prisoners of War with thousands of other prisoners.

Two ABs including myself, the carpenter and bosun [F. J. Bennett] were called to the office to give an account of the capture of the ship. It was all taken down as a statement and we had to sign it. The next thing we heard was that we had to go to Bruges for the Captain's trial. We went at night and were shoved into prison cells. Next morning they took us out under army escort, and they marched us to the town hall of Bruges for the trial.

The judge was an army man. The jury were naval men and the interpreter was the commander in charge of the flotilla which stopped us. I was the first witness called in. They threatened us that if we ran away they would shoot. After the trial was over we heard the Captain would be sentenced at 5.00 p.m. on the same day. They sent for the mate to spend the last hour with Captain Fryatt* because he was going to be shot at 7.00 p.m. but we didn't know anything about it till next morning.

During that evening I got a pack of cards and was playing patience in my cell, when about 7.00 p.m. one of the army brass bands struck up. I thought it was another crowd going to the front. It wasn't, it was the time for shooting poor old Captain Fryatt. The band was to deaden the volley I expect.

Next morning we went into the yard, and then the mate told us about spending the last hour with the Captain[*]. They kept us there for about four days. We eventually went back to the town near Berlin [¶] and, in the meantime, the Battle of Jutland was on the go. They brought survivors from that battle to the same camp where we were.

Then they made us military Prisoners of War, and they sent us to Brandenburg. There were plenty of Russians and French, all PoWs. We were sent out on commando – a company of about 12 men to different places. The commando I was put in was sent to the edge of the Black Forest to chop down trees. It was near Christmas time. Some of the men went into the salt mines and some on the railway. We got in such a weak state in the forest because they couldn't feed us, that they sent us back to Brandenburg. Parcels sent to us were getting smashed up.

They sent us to Premnitz to work outside a gunpowder factory. We were under strict guard all the time, and during the time we were there we had a flu epidemic. After a time they sent us back to Brandenburg, and from there I went on the railway to work. At the finish there was more or less revolution in the German army, and they looked after us.

Records show that a few of the crew were released prematurely in 1918, namely First Engineer Thurlow, Chief Steward Tovill and AB H. Gilbert on 27 February, and First Officer Hartnell on 16 May. Steward G. P. Carter and AB J .J. Wyatt are recorded as having died in captivity.

After the Armistice George Calver was repatriated, first to Scotland where a band on the quayside welcomed the party home, then to his home in Pepys Street, Harwich. On 8 July 1919 he was in the procession in London for Captain Fryatt's memorial service at St Paul's Cathedral and later that day at his reburial at Dovercourt. Eventually he became a Harwich borough councillor and was the town's first Labour alderman.

§ **Ymuiden**
A port about forty miles north-east along the coast from the Hook at the entrance to the canal linking Amsterdam with the North Sea.

¶**Ruhleben**
A racecourse on a 20-acre site in a western suburb of Berlin, where British and Allied civilians were interned from November 1914. There was a total of around 5,500 prisoners but, with comings and goings, the average at any one time was about 5,000. The internees comprised people living or studying in Germany at the outbreak of war, crews of merchant ships captured at sea or stranded in German ports and fishermen whose boats had been sunk by enemy action.

Many of the prisoners were housed in the stables, six to a stall. Initially conditions were very bad, with one cold water tap in each, no heating or proper bedding and little lighting.

Brussels's crew logging party, based at Brandenburg PoW camp but probably working in the Black Forest. (Bob Clow Collection)

Brussels crew football team, as PoWs at Ruhleben. (Bob Clow Collection)

Brussels crew gathered informally at Ruhleben. (*GER Magazine*)

However, following the intervention of the American ambassador, James W. Gerrard (see Chapter 2), during that first winter the Germans started to adhere to the Geneva convention and matters greatly improved.

The captors then took a fairly relaxed stance towards their prisoners, who were allowed to run their lives along fairly autonomous lines. Among other things they organised their own sport, policing, library, magazines, theatre and even a casino; initially there was a postal system but this was outlawed by the German postal authority and had to be closed down. A collective appraisal recorded at the end of the war stated, 'Although unable to fight for our King and Country on the battlefield we endeavoured to maintain the British ideal of patriotism, patience, courage and usefulness through four years'.

*Apparently some confusion here between William Hartnell and the German naval chaplain (see Appendix D).

Appendix D

Letters

Contained here are copies of various letters to Mrs Fryatt shortly before and after her husband's death. The letters from Captain Fryatt and Chaplain Köhne are reproduced courtesy Harwich Town Council Archives.

Copy of Captain Fryatt's last letter to his family, not received until just after his execution.

This was taken from a copy of the original manuscript, which understandably had become rather indistinct over the course of time, but is reproduced here as closely as possible with permission also from Julian Luckett:

1 July 1916

Dear Wife & Children

Just a few more lines hoping they will find you all doing well as this leaves me doing well at the present. I sent you a letter so I expect you have got it by this time to let you know I was alright. I have to go away on business and I may be away for over a week so if you don't hear from me don't get alarmed. I shall write as soon as I can to you so you must be content to wait. I shall be quite alright. I expect you all have been very anxious about me but it might have been worse. It cannot be helped now. It is the fortunes of war.

I expect the children miss me and also yourself, but times will change. Take care of the children, the Company will no doubt look after you and the children. Remember me to all inquiring friends. When you send the parcel don't forget to address it right and put it in a cardboard box. I only want some flannel shirts, under shirts and I will let you know when to send me anything else and send some soap and also send some pills and also anything you think I might want. No papers to be sent and no news of any sort concerning the war, only about yourself and children.

So now my dear I will finish

So with kind love I remain your ever loving husband

(signed) C. *Fryatt*

My address to put on parcel and letters
 Charles Fryatt
 British Civil P of War
 Barracke 1 Box 15
 Ruhleben
 Care of GPO London

Kiss all the family for me and Charles will give you one for me. Tell him to be a good boy and to go to school until I come home again and then Father will buy him something. I hope the girls will take great care of you my dear while I am away and don't worry yourself about anything until I return. Take things easy. That will be the time when Dad comes home again.

So good bye and God bless you all
XXXXX

Copy of letter dated 3 August 1916 from German Lutheran Naval Chaplain Köhne to Mrs Fryatt, shortly after Captain Fryatt's execution:

Dear Madam
 No doubt you have meanwhile heard of the death of your husband on 27th July by judgement of a duly instituted Court Martial.
 As I spent his last moments with him, in order to prepare him for his fateful journey, he naturally spoke to me of you and his children; he begged me to convey to you and them his last goodbye and tell you how he died. This I do willingly as follows:
 I met your husband calm and resigned in his room. I told him he had to prepare for his doom and appear before his heavenly judge. He knew what he had done, and thought by doing so, to do something for his country. He had to bear the penalty for his deed which, according to the laws of war, could not be passed over by us. He acknowledged it with a nod, and said he took it all upon himself. We then prayed together out of the Book of Common Prayer, read the 23rd Psalm; he promised me to be brave to the end.
 Overshadowed by beautiful trees he spoke again much of you and of his children. He told me their names and expressed the hope that that they, especially the elder ones, would stand by their mother and help her in her great bereavement. To all, and above [all] to yourself, he sends his best love. As his last hour had come, we spoke again of God, before whom he was about to appear, and hoped to be forgiven for his wrongdoings. He then asked me where his body would rest; I told him that it would be committed to the Belgian authorities and buried in the Bruges cemetery. He begged me, if possible, to send you a photo of his grave, which I shall be pleased to do, if allowed. After a last prayer, which we said together, he met his death calmly.
 Now I beg to send you and your children a word of consolation. May you bear this terrible blow, and tell yourself, as your husband did, that it is the consequence of a deed punishable by the laws of war. He thought he had a right to act as he did for the sake

of his country, and has suffered death for it. Let us hope that God, to whom he has resigned, has received him in his mercy.

May the Almighty and Merciful help you and your children.

(signed) *Köhne*,
Naval Chaplain

Bruges 3/VIII/1916

Facsimile letter from the King's private secretary to Mrs Fryatt following the execution.

BUCKINGHAM PALACE

2nd. August 1916.

Madam,

In the sorrow which has so cruelly stricken you the King joins with his people in offering you his heartfelt sympathy.

Since the outbreak of the War His Majesty has followed with admiration the splendid services of the Mercantile Marine.

The action of Captain Fryatt in defending his ship against the attack of an enemy submarine was a noble instance of the resource and self-reliance so characteristic of that profession.

It is therefore with feelings of the deepest indignation that the King learnt of your husband's fate, and in conveying to you the expression of his condolence I am commanded to assure you of the abhorrence with which His Majesty regards this outrage.

Yours very faithfully,

Stamfordham

Mrs Fryatt.

Appendix E

Legalities and Rationale

The arguments over the legalities of both the Germans' and Fryatt's actions persisted until long after the war, and the debate remains even today. International law at the time allowed passengers and crews to escape from a captured merchant ship before it was sunk. However, it was a dangerous procedure for a submarine, which once surfaced could be outrun, rammed or fired upon by other armed vessels. Furthermore, unless survivors were left to take their chances in lifeboats, they could not be accommodated in the cramped quarters of a submarine, neither could U-boat captains afford prize crews to take captured merchantmen and their passengers and crews into captivity. They therefore put their vessels and crews at great risk in attempting to observe the accepted rules of war.

On 18 September 1915, six months after the German declaration of unrestricted submarine warfare, the Kaiser was forced to rescind it on account of adverse world opinion, especially from America. In a further twist, however, unrestricted submarine warfare was resumed on 1 April 1916 and lasted until the end of October 1918, shortly before the Armistice.

In view of the worldwide outrage resulting from the *Brussels* affair, the Germans naturally tried to justify their actions on the international stage. Their rather spurious argument was that the British insisted that merchant ships had the right to attack submarines without warning, while it refused to concede the same right to submarines. They further claimed that the British had disregarded the fact that lives aboard the *Brussels* had been spared, and she had turned against *U-33* without warning. Of the greatest significance, however, was that Fryatt was a civilian non-combatant and as such had become a *franc-tireur*, which the Germans claimed had always been punishable by death in both land and sea warfare.

The British reply was that, since *U-33* was attempting to attack the *Brussels* without warning, which in itself would have been a violation of international law, Fryatt was acting in self-defence. The USA, which prided itself on its respect for the law, agreed with Britain in concluding that it was the privilege of merchant seamen to defend themselves when threatened on the high seas, although the Germans claimed that this did not apply to attacks by submarines.

Fryatt's death arose from a fundamental disagreement between the warring nations as to the status of merchant ships in wartime. The Germans always defied the Anglo-American stance that merchant ships had an inherent right to defend themselves from enemy attack, which had been recognised internationally for centuries. Early U-boats could not carry many torpedoes and being on the surface made them vulnerable to attack, both by surface warships and ramming by unarmed merchant ships. No wonder the Germans insisted that merchant ships had no right to self-defence, since the exercise of such a right would endanger their U-boats.

At this stage of the conflict, submarine warfare was still, relatively speaking, in its infancy and there remained a lack of clear-cut rules as to its conduct. The extensive use of German U-boats throughout the war provoked worldwide unpopularity, yet Britain still 'ruled the waves' and they were the best weapons at the Germans' disposal by which they could both break the British blockade, which was causing them great hardship, and also impose their own blockade on Britain. Yet they were aware of the unpopularity of their submarines and were keen to improve world opinion of them. This might explain, at least in part, the delay of nearly fifteen months before they captured Fryatt and his ship, which was probably timed to coincide with the visit of their merchant submarine *Deutschland* to America (see Appendix G).

Meanwhile, as far as wartime service was concerned, was Captain Fryatt a civilian? The Germans, of course, said he was, largely because he was wearing a company's livery rather than a standard service uniform. After the war, a standard officers' uniform was introduced by virtue of the British Mercantile Marine Uniform Act 1919, so that, in the event of another war, the MM, shortly to be renamed the Merchant Navy, would automatically become one of the Services. Thus the merchant service would be protected against incidents such as the one which cost Captain Fryatt his life.

Appendix F

Captain Fryatt Railway Locomotive

In January 1913 the London & North Western Railway had introduced the 'Claughton' Class 4-6-0 express passenger locomotives, which were built until June 1921. The class was designed by Charles Bowen Cooke and named in honour of Sir Gilbert Claughton, who was then chairman of the LNWR. Only 57 of the 120 locomotives were named and the thirty-second locomotive, which entered service in March 1917, was numbered 154 and named *Captain Fryatt*. Three later locomotives were named after company employees who had won the Victoria Cross during the war.

On Railway Grouping at midnight on 31 December 1922, No. 154 was transferred to the London Midland & Scottish Railway (LMS), but not renumbered 5931 and given LMS livery until April 1926. In May 1926 she was converted to oil burning to meet the coal shortages during the General Strike, but was soon converted back to coal. No. 5931 was withdrawn from service in March 1934; none of the class was preserved and, to date, neither of the *Captain Fryatt* nameplates, if either survived, has come to light despite extensive enquiries.

It was unusual, although not unique, for a railway company to name one of its locomotives after a member or employee of another company, both before or after Grouping (the GER became part of the LNER, which was an arch rival of the LMS, which incorporated the L&NWR) but such was the strength of feeling about the war at the time that such differences appear to have been of little concern.

Appendix G

German Merchant Submarines

Deutschland was the first of seven projected unarmed merchant submarines designed to break the British shipping blockade of Germany. The name, however, should not be confused with that of the 1931 German pocket battleship *Deutschland*, sister ship to the *Admiral Graf Spee* of December 1939 Battle of the River Plate notoriety. The later *Deutschland* was renamed *Lützow* in November 1939.

With a displacement of 2,272 tons, the submarines could carry 750 tons of cargo but only two vessels were completed. Launched at the Flensburger Schiffbau yard in March 1916, *Deutschland* first sailed from Kiel, fully laden under Merchant Marine Kpt. Paul König, on 23 June 1916. She arrived at Baltimore on 9 July (USA was then still neutral), although not without first being the subject of various sightings in the Atlantic, but evading interception by the Royal Navy. Notwithstanding the anti-German feelings arising from the sinking of the *Lusitania* the previous year, she received a surprising welcome by the Americans, who enthused over the design concept. On 2 August, *Deutschland* sailed laden with rubber, mostly as deck cargo, nickel and tin, which were all vital war supplies. After running the RN gauntlet again she arrived home on 24 August, having covered 8,450 sea miles, of which 190 critical miles were submerged.

It became clear after *Deutschland*'s first merchant venture that there were still strong pro-German feelings in America, doubtless backed by commercial considerations, which would be a formidable obstacle in the way of the Allies bringing the US into the war. However, the whole ploy, designed primarily to counter any elements of Germany's bad reputation in the US, was short-lived. After a second commercial return voyage, this time to New London, Connecticut, *Deutschland* was armed with guns and torpedo tubes and, in February 1917, drafted into the German navy as *U-155*. She was involved in several actions and sinkings over the next twenty-one months, then surrendered at Harwich under the terms of the Armistice in November 1918. She was then sold by the Admiralty to James Dredging in March 1919 for exhibition in London (at Tower Bridge), Great Yarmouth, Southend, Ramsgate, Brighton and Douglas (IoM), before being sold on to John Bull Ltd and broken up at Birkenhead in 1921.

Meanwhile the second and final commercial submarine, the *Bremen*, which sailed from Bremerhaven for Norfolk, Virginia, in September 1916, seems to have disappeared unaccountably on her maiden voyage. Records vary as to her demise, some versions saying she was rammed or struck by the ex-P&O Armed Merchant Cruiser HMS *Mantua* between Shetland and Iceland, while others claim she was torpedoed by the submarine

G13. There remains a school of thought, however, that she survived the torpedo hit and returned to port, where she was written off as a submarine and converted to a surface vessel. In the absence of any positive evidence, however, it is equally likely that she hit a mine.

It is interesting to note that *U-155*'s sister ship *U-156*, which had been built as, rather than converted to, a 'Deutschland'-class submarine, was commanded by Konrad Gansser between commissioning in August 1917 and the end of that year. She was eventually presumed to have been sunk by a mine in August 1918 in the Northern Barrage, a chain of Allied minefields between the Orkney and Faroe Islands and extending to Iceland.

Appendix H

Funeral of Captain Fryatt at Dovercourt

A summary of Harwich General Orders issued by Rear Admiral Charles F. Thorp, Senior Naval Officer representing the Admiralty, dated 29 June 1919.

After the funeral service at St Paul's Cathedral, the coffin would leave Liverpool Street station at 2 p.m. on 8 July by special train, arriving at Dovercourt Bay station between 3.30 and 4.00 p.m. (in fact it arrived at 3.35 p.m.). Here the procession would be drawn up in a large semicircle on Kingsway and Station Road, skirting round the Victoria Hotel, with the gun carriage opposite the station entrance. The lower length of Kingsway would be lined by a naval party, two deep on either side with seniors nearest the station, and a similar formation by military personnel along the upper length. The whole formation was to be ready in place by 3.00 p.m.

Twelve strong men from the HMS *Ganges* (Royal Navy Training Establishment, Shotley – opposite Harwich on the other side of the river), commanded by a senior rank, were detailed to act as bearers and pall-bearers, to remove the coffin from the train, place it on the gun carriage and then take up their positions either side. The procession comprised:

- Police, to ensure the way clear
- Shotley Band
- Buglers
- Local Friendly Society representatives
- Mercantile Marine representatives
- Gun Carriage (drawn by six black horses)
- Carriages for Relatives
- Vehicle for Wreaths
- Carriages for GER Officials
- Carriages for Mayor and Corporation [Representatives]
- Carriage for Senior Naval Officer and Staff
- Carriages for Local Civic Representatives

As the procession moved off, the military and naval parties would fall in at the rear, four abreast, with the former in front.

The route of the procession was up Kingsway, then as far as the monument at the end of Marine Parade, all in slow time, then breaking into quick time on entering Fronks Road. At Pounds Farm (junction of Fronks Road and Main Road), the procession would pause to allow the clergy to take their places in front of the gun carriage, before proceeding along the short distance to the church.

On arrival at the lychgate, the following instructions had been issued for respective parties:

- Shotley Band to move along the road past the gate and remain outside until after the burial.
- Buglers to proceed down the path and form up in line against the hedge beyond the grave.
- Friendly Society and Mercantile Marine representatives to proceed through the gate and line the path to the grave. As soon as the local civil representatives had passed down the path they were to follow the procession and spread out when they had reached the open space around the grave.
- The military and naval parties to divide into two columns and follow the Friendly Society and Mercantile Marine representatives into the churchyard, officers leading.
- Immediately after the burial the buglers to sound Last Post and march out of the churchyard ahead of the military and naval parties, officers in front.
- After the ceremony the Shotley Band will lead the remainder of the procession back by Main Road.

Two groups had been detailed to arrive at the churchyard ahead of the procession, with the path down the churchyard and around the grave to be kept clear by local Scouts. In addition the Great Eastern Railway Band (in fact the massed bands of the Cambridge, March and Stratford Railways) to assemble at the grave before the arrival of the procession and play suitable music beforehand, then music for the burial service.

The original parade diagram showed the relatives' carriage followed by the GER officials, which in turn would be ahead of the wreaths' vehicle. The text of the orders, however, stated that the vehicle would be placed immediately behind the relatives' carriage. In any case the wreaths' vehicle was to be in the charge of a Petty Officer and six ratings, again from *Ganges*, detailed to be on the platform before the arrival of the train and to attend to the wreaths, both at the station and in the churchyard.

The photograph in Chapter 5, taken on the corner of Marine Parade and Lee Road shows the bishops already in the procession, although it is not clear where they joined it. This was clearly a variation of the Harwich Order.

<u>Author's Note</u>: Apart from the bishops' instructions, it is not known how much, if at all, the original orders were varied on the day. It has been assumed, rightly or wrongly, that they were followed fairly closely, with perhaps the occasional detailed variation due to changed circumstances.

A Few of the Author's Thoughts on the Organisation of the Repatriation

Although records of the preparations are sparse, consideration should be given to the logistical achievement of the events over the five days between 4 and 8 July 1919, in two different countries without a common language. In Belgium there would have been the need for approval for disinterring the body, two formal processions (Bruges and Antwerp), train between the two cities, use of the RN ships, the procession in Dover, the South Eastern & Chatham Railway to bring the body to London, the procession to St Paul's, organisation of the cathedral service followed by a further procession to Liverpool Street station, the in-house funeral train to Dovercourt and the procession and burial there. The combined operations throughout involved, *inter alia*, numerous civil organisations and businesses, the Mercantile Marine, the Police, Church, at least two railway companies in England and one in Belgium, thousands of Army and Navy personnel, numerous service and civilian bandsmen and probably hundreds of horses and vehicles of all kinds.

It is not known when arrangements were started. Records show that the music was rehearsed 'for several months', which could have meant since the Armistice the previous November. On the other hand, Fryatt's brother William did not leave the Army until May 1919, so may not have been completely free until well after the Armistice. Nevertheless, it is amazing how so many events were coordinated within such a short period, with the relatively primitive communications of the day. As far as Dovercourt was concerned, for example, the Harwich General Orders of 29 June above were issued barely ten days before the event.

Appendix I

Abbreviations

B&ISPCo	British & Irish Steam Packet Company
D&LSSCo	Dublin & Lancashire Steam Ship Co
GCR	Great Central Railway
GER	Great Eastern Railway
grt	Gross registered tonnage (see 'Ship Tonnages' below)
IWM	Imperial War Museum
K&ESR	Kent & East Sussex Railway
LMS	London Midland & Scottish (Railway)
LNER	London & North Eastern Railway
LNWR	London & North Western Railway
LSMT	Liverpool Scottish Museum Trust
PoW	Prisoner(s) of War
RA	Royal Artillery
RM	Royal Marine(s)
RN	Royal Navy
RNR	Royal Navy Reserve
RNVR	Royal Navy Volunteer Reserve
SE&CR	South Eastern & Chatham Railway
SS	Steam Ship

Ship Tonnages

Statistics are shown primarily for guidance and comparison purposes. Tonnages indicated for commercial shipping are gross, which usually have little bearing on actual weights; grt is an artificial standard of measurement, based on total volume of enclosed space within a ship (100 cubic feet = one ton). Net tonnage is based on revenue-earning space and calculated by deducting non-revenue-earning space such as for navigation, machinery, fuel, stores and crew accommodation, and it is on net tonnage that port, canal and such dues are payable.

By contrast tonnages for warships, which do not, of course, carry commercial passengers or freight, are displacement weights based on the Archimedes principle of weight of water displaced by a floating mass, i.e. 35 cubic feet of sea water weighing approximately one ton.

Royal Navy Reserve/Royal Navy Volunteer Reserve

Confusion sometimes arises between the two reserve services. The RNR was founded in 1859 and comprised officers and ratings of the Mercantile Marine (renamed Merchant Navy after the war), who underwent periodic training with the Royal Navy, usually in their employers' time, ready to serve in the event of war. Cuff rings denoting officer ranks were of interwoven chain pattern.

The RNVR was formed in 1903 and ran more on the lines of the Territorial Force (since 1920 known as the Territorial Army and now the Army Reserve), with members from all walks of life training in their spare time and ready to mobilise when necessary. Officer cuff rings in waves often gave rise to the nickname 'Wavy Navy' but, with a few exceptions and modifications, these were converted to plain RN style in 1952. In 1958 the two services merged and continued under the RNR title.

Maps

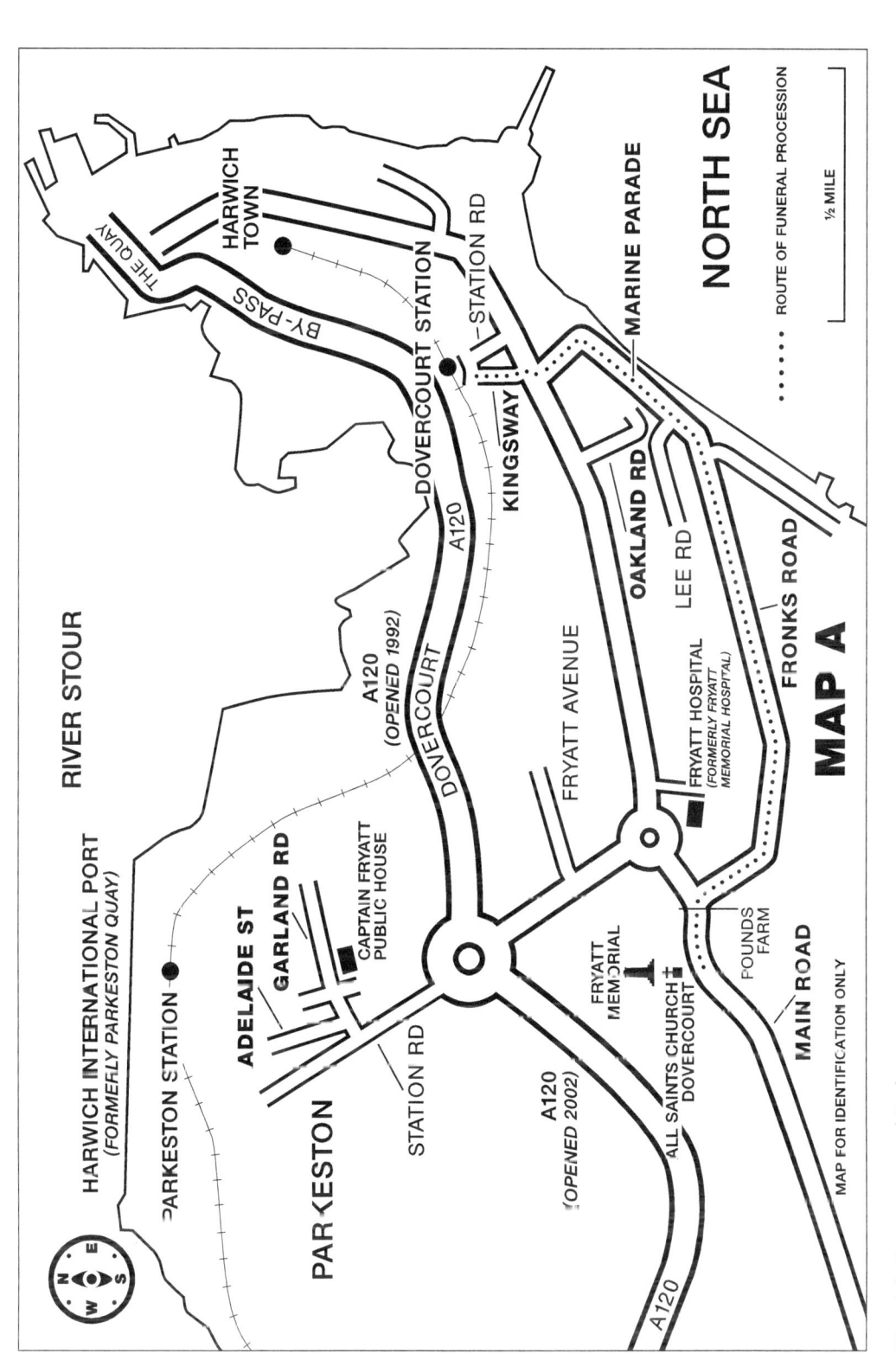

Harwich, Dovercourt and Parkeston.

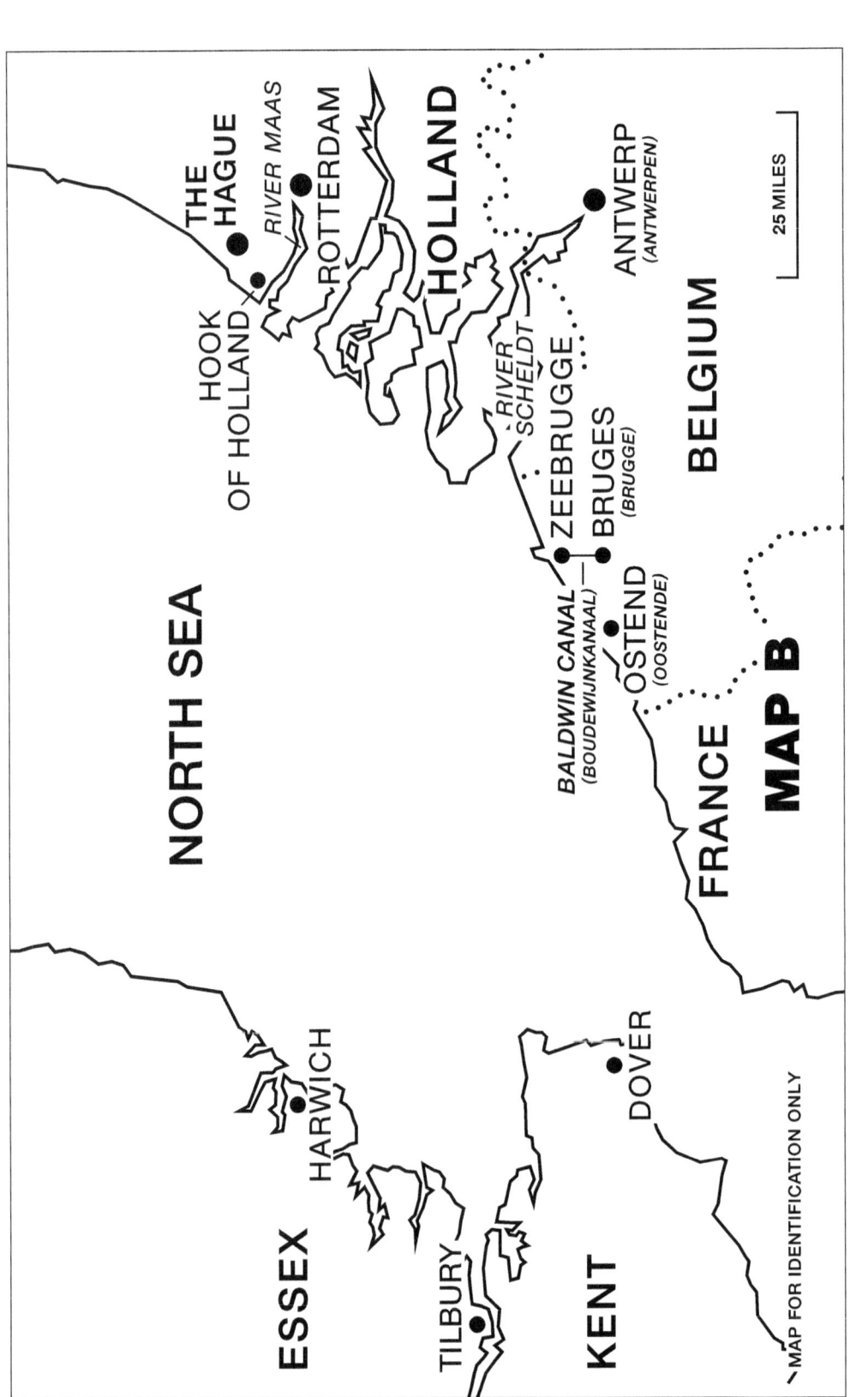

North Sea.

MAP C

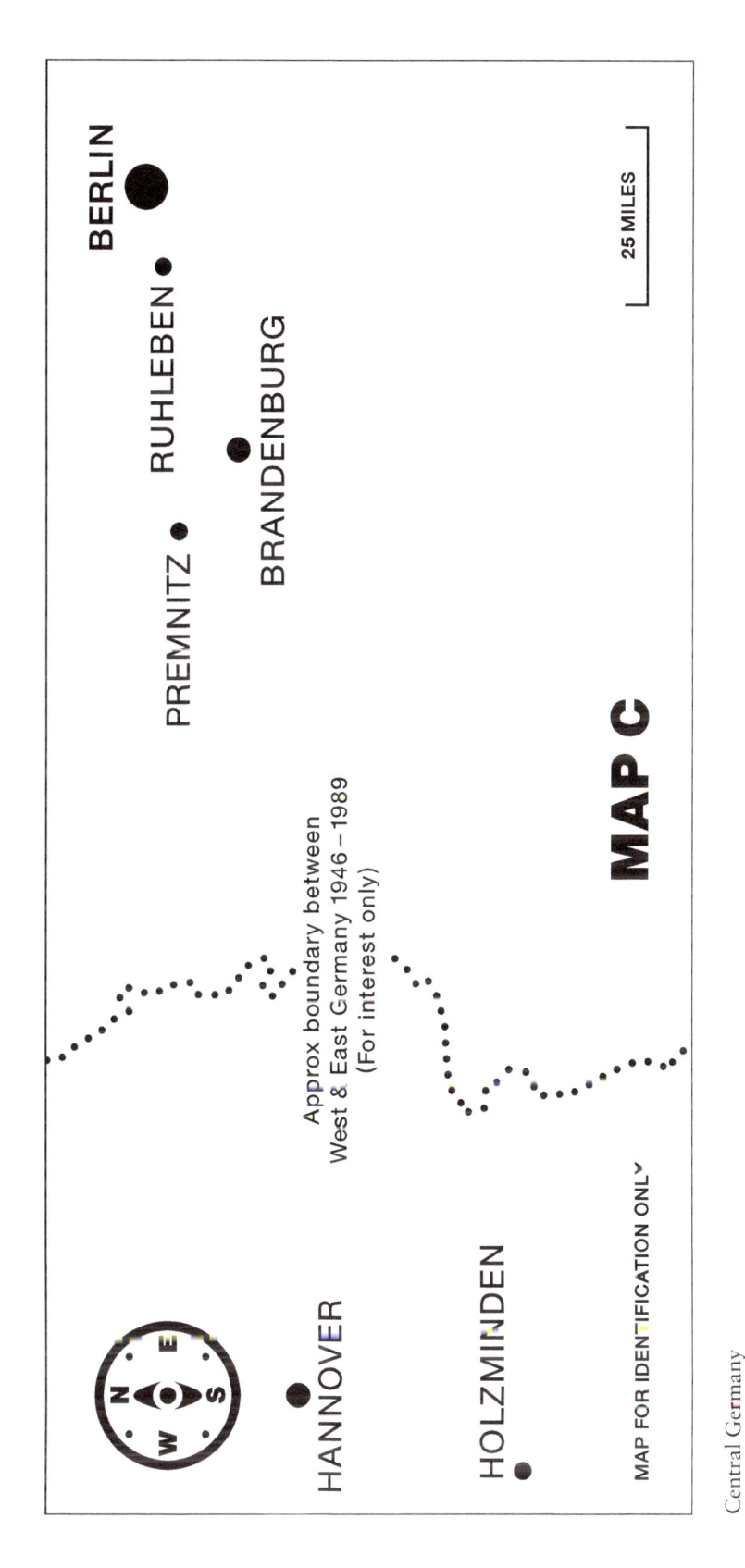

MAP FOR IDENTIFICATION ONLY

- BERLIN
- RUHLEBEN
- PREMNITZ
- BRANDENBURG
- HANNOVER
- HOLZMINDEN

Approx boundary between West & East Germany 1946–1989 (For interest only)

25 MILES

Central Germany
Map illustrations by Graham May of Maycreation Graphic Design; www.maycreation.co.uk

Bibliography

Algernon, Charles, *The Murder of Captain Fryatt* (1916). (Whitefish, USA: Kessinger Publishing, 2011 – republication of a booklet first published by Hodder and Stoughton, London 1916).
Bridgland, Tony, *Outrage at Sea – Naval Atrocities in the First World War* (Barnsley: Leo Cooper/Pen & Sword Books, 2002).
Crozier, Joseph, *In the Enemy's Country* (London: Hutchinson & Co., 1931).
Dawson, Charles, *Captain Charles Fryatt and the 'Brussels'* (Liverpool Nautical Research Society bulletin, c. 1998).
Deseyne, Alex, *Battlefield Tourism on the Coast after WW1* (Ostend: Flanders Marine Institute, *Der Grote Rede*, 2013).
Ferguson, Niall, *The Pity of War* (NY: Basic Books, 1999).
GER Magazine, various issues from July 1916 to June 1920.
Gray, Adrian, *Hero – or War Criminal?* (St Leonards-on-Sea: HPC Publishing, *Shipping Today and Yesterday* magazine, 2009).
Grehan, John, 'Dammed if You Do and Dead if You Don't', *Britain at War* magazine (2007).
Hall, Phyllis, 'Pirate or Patriot – The Strange Case of Captain Fryatt', *History Today* magazine (1988).
Hurd, Sir Archibald, *History of the Great War – The Merchant Navy Vol. 2* (London: John Murray, 1924)
Leonard, Alan, 'Captain Charles Fryatt – Pirate Dodger of WW1', *Picture Postcard Monthly* (1989).
Light, John P., 'An Immortal Shipmaster', *Sea Breezes* magazine (1950).
McRonald, Malcolm, *The Irish Boats Vol. 1* (Stroud: Tempus Publishing, 2005).
Parsons, Alan, *Captain Charles Algernon Fryatt – Master of SS 'Brussels'* (Harwich: published privately, c. 1990).
Roberts, Hamish, 'The Case of Captain Fryatt in the Great War', *Master Mariners* magazine (2011).
Simmonds, Capt. W.H. 'How the Merchant Navy Got its Uniform', *Ocean Mail* magazine.
Talbot-Booth RNR and Paymr, E.C., *Merchant Ships* (London: Sampson Low, Marston & Co., 1937).
Toms, George and Essary, Bob, *Claughton & Patriot 4-6-0s* (Didcot: Wild Swan Publications, 2006).

White, Michael G., *Captain Fryatt – Patriot or Pirate* (Southampton: published by Author, 2005).

Winchester, Clarence (ed.), *Shipping Wonders of the World* (London: Amalgamated Press, 1936).

Acknowledgements

In addition to those credited in the Preface, I would like to thank the following for their assistance in preparing this book (in surname alphabetical order):
John Avery – Southampton Fryatt Plaque
Mark Baker – General assistance with research
Lucy Ballard – Harwich Town Council
Kevin Barnett and Pauline Lodwidge – Freemantle Church of England Community Academy, Southampton
Mike Bolton – Photograph restorations
Tony Booth – Advice on legalities and financial implications of *Brussels*'s salvage
Lewis Brockway – Photographer to the Kent & East Sussex Railway
Michelle Cooper – Assistant Keeper, Lancashire Maritime Museum, Lancaster
Barrie Duncan - South Lanarkshire Leisure & Culture Ltd (Scottish Rifles)
Dr Noël Geirnaert – Bruges City Archivist
Jean Holland – General assistance with photographic images
Neville Hyde and Raymond Kearns – Corporate Adviser and Operations Manager respectively, Centreport, Wellington, NZ
Alan Jeffreys – Imperial War Museum (Fryatt medals)
David Jones and Geoff Burton – GC Railwayana over painting of SS *Wrexham*
Benoit Kervyn – Bruges Museum Service
Bill King – Chairman GER Society
Norman Lee, Dave Pennington and Neil Burgess – LNWR Society
Malcolm McRonald – Further assistance with book *The Irish Boats*
Linda Morgan – Assistant Archivist, Harwich Society
Dennis Reeves – Curator Liverpool Scottish Museum Trust, Liverpool
Garry Wemyss – South Tyneside Council Local Studies Library
Christine Shuttleworth and Dominic George – Harris Library, Preston
Joke Simoen – Bruges Tourism Dept
Annette Speed – Captain Charles Fryatt Memorial Fund
Celia Strachan – Assistance with the Fryatt Hospital
Hannah Thomas – Librarian RHS Wisley
Maeve Underwood – Imperial War Museum (Fryatt watches)
Willy Vereenooghe – Bruges local photographer
Simon Wallis – Cambridge University Botanic Gardens (Fryatt tulip)

Andrew Walmsley – Community History Librarian, St Annes-on-Sea Library
Joseph Wisdom – Librarian, St Paul's Cathedral

In addition I am indebted to various individuals and organisations for trying to find information, but without success.

Index

Adams, Ric 11
Adder (dockyard launch) 48
Adelaide Advertiser 35
Admiral Graf Spee (German pocket battleship) Appendix G
Admiralty 18, 20, 21, 26, 27, 37, 51, 76, 78, Note 21, Appendix A, H
Adriatic (Sea) 75
Aisne, Battle of the Note 14
Algernon, Charles Note 7
Allies 18, 77, 78, Note 10, Appendix G
America/USA 23, 30, 62 Note 7, Appendix E, G
Antwerp, City of 17, 18, 39, 44–45, 46, Note 12, 13, Appendix E
  Middenstatie Station 44
Archangel 76
Ardrossan 76
Argentine Appendix B
Armistice 74, Appendix E, G
Army Reserve Appendix I
Asquith, Prime Minister Herbert 30
Atlantic (Ocean) Appendix G
Australia 62, Appendix A
Azores Straat 62

Baldwin Canal 23, Map B
Baltimore Appendix G
Banks, Monte 11
Barenedorf, Kapitänleutnant Appendix B
Barking, Bishop of 54, 68, Note 19
Barren, Captain 51
Beeching, Captain F. 18

Belgian Maritime Cross 34, Note 8
Belgium/Belgian(s) 18, 22, 23, 37, 62, 72, 77, Map B, Notes 11, 16, 17 Appendix D
Bell, Guild Mayor of Preston H.A. 41, 42
Ben Cruachan, SS 18
Bennett, Bosun F.J. Appendix C
Berlin 23, 29, Appendix C, Map C
Birkenhead Appendix G
Birkett, Cdr M. B. DSO 45
Black Forest Appendix C
Black Sea 75
Blockade Appendix E
Blue Ensign 40
Blyth 75
Board of Trade 51
Bolsheviks 76
Book of Common Prayer Appendix D
Bowen Cooke, Charles Appendix F
Brandenburg Appendix C, Map C
Bremen Appendix G
Bremerhaven Appendix G
Brighton Appendix G
Bristol Channel 76
Britain/British 17, 18, 39, 75, Note 13, 14, Appendix E, G
  Embassy 77
  Empire (Union) 30, Appendix D
  War Medal 35, Note 8
  Workers League 30
British & Irish Steam Packet Co. 41, Note 13
Brooks, Lt R. 38
Bruce, Vera Note 9

Bruges (Brugge), City of 23, 28, 29, 72,
    Note 5, 16, Appendix C, Map B
  Assebroek Cemetery 28, 43, Appendix D
  Beluik der Gefusilleerden 27, **66**
  English Convent 65
  Hof van Aurora 27, 65, 68, 77
  Provinciaal Hof 25, **26**, 44, 70
Bruges, SS 75, **75**
Brussels Peak 65
Brussels, SS 7, **17**, 18, 20-22, 23, 26, 54,
    60, 65, 68, 69, 72, 77, 78, Note 10, 13,
    19, 20, 21, Appendix C, E
  Stewardesses (by name) Note 4
Bryant, Captain F.H. DSC 40
Buckingham Palace Appendix D
Bütlar, General Freiherr von 27

Cabinet, The 51
Calver, AB G.A. Appendix C
Cambridge
  Railway Band 54
Cameronia, SS 76
Canberra, Australia Note 9
Cannock Chase Military Cemetery 76
Captain Charles Fryatt Memorial
  Fund Note 11
Captain Fryatt
  Patriot or Pirate (book) 11
  Remembered (Exhibition) 70, **71, 72**
  Steam locomotive 32, Appendix F
Cardiff 18
Carter, Steward G.P. Appendix C
Carver, Meriel 12
Chalet Fryatt 69
Chasseurs Alpins 45
Chatham 48
  RM Band 48
Chavanga 76
Chelmsford, Bishop of 54
China 78
Claud Hamilton (locomotive) Note 15
Claud Hamilton Locomotive
  Group Note 18
Claughton, Sir Gilbert Appendix F
Clow, Bob 11

Clyde, River 41, 76
Colchester, Bishop of 54
Colchester, SS 17, 77
Cologne 23
Constantinople 75
Coysh, Cdr 60
Crozier, Joseph Note 21
de Villiers, British Ambassador Sir Francis
    40, 44, 45
Descheppen, Councillor 27
Deutschland (German merchant
    submarine) 78, Appendix E
Ditchford, Diocesan Bishop John 54
Douglas, IoM Appendix G
Dover Map B
  General Officer Commanding 48
  Harbour 48
  Infantry Garrison 48
  Marine Station 48
  Patrol 48
  Procession 48, **49**
Dovercourt
  All Saints Church 54, 70, **70**, 72,
     Appendix H, Map A
  Fronks Road 54, Appendix H, Map A
  Fryatt Memorial see *Fryatt*
  Kingsway 54, Appendix H, Map A
  Lee Road Appendix H, Map A
  Main Road 54, Appendix H, Map A
  Marine Parade 54, Appendix H, Map A
  Oakland Road 17, Map A
  Pounds Farm Appendix H, Map A
  Station 51, Appendix H, Map A
  Station Road Appendix H, Map A
  Victoria Road Appendix H, Map A
Dragon, HMS 40
Dublin 40, 41
Dublin & Lancashire Steam Ship Co. 40

Ellenbank, SV 14
Elwood, Chief Stewardess Mrs Alice 22,
    Note 4
England/English 62
English Channel Note 10
Enigma (coding machine) 76

Eskimo, SS 40
Essex Regiment Note 14
Eternal Father Strong to Save (hymn) 45

Falaba, SS 20
Far East 78
Farmer & Hindley, Messrs 54
Faroe Is. Appendix G
Farthing,
    Harry Appendix A
    Helen Appendix A
    Tom Appendix A
Flanders/Flemish 27, 29
Flensburger Schiffbau (shipyard) Appendix G
Forbes tartan 44
Fox, Chief Constable D.H. 48
France/French 27, 75, Note 21, Appendix C, Map B
Franc-tireur Appendix E
Freemantle, C of E Community Academy 14, 15, 70, Note 1
Frestone, Telegraphist J. 23
Friendly Society Appendix H
Fryatt, Captain Charles Algernon 17, 18, 20, 21, 22, 23, 226, 28, 30, 31, 31, 37, 38, 77, 78 Note 6, 21, Appendix A, C, D, E
    Capture 22, 28
    Court martial 13, 23, 25 27, Note 6, Appendix D
    Childhood 14
    Disinterment 43, **43**, 44
    Early career 14-21
    Execution 13, 27-29, 78
    Grave/Memorial 55, 56, 57, 58, Appendix H
    Imprisonment 23
    Medals 32, Note 8
    Memorial Service 50, 51
    Reburial 54-57, Appendix H
    Repatriation 44-48
    Watches 19, 21, 21, 26, Appendix A
Fryatt, Algernon Percy (brother) 14
    Bessie Sophia (sister) 14
    Charles (father) 14

Charles Algernon Sidney (son) 17, **33**, 60, Appendix D
Doris Irene (daughter) 14, Appendix A
Dorothy Ada Mary (daughter) 9, 17, Appendix A
Elizabeth Annie Jane (sister) 14
Ethel, née Townend (wife) 14, **16**, 27, 28, 31, **33**, Appendix A, D
John Algernon (brother) 14
Mabel Marjorie (daughter) 17
Mary Caroline (sister) 14
Mary Jane Brown, *née* Percy (mother) 14
Olive Anne (daughter) 14, Appendix A
William Percy (brother) 14, 44, 45, 48, **67**, Note 11
Fryatt Hospital & Mayflower Medical Centre 60, **61**, **62**, **63**
Funeral March (Chopin) 44

G101-4 (German destroyers) Appendix B
G13 (British submarine) Appendix G
Gale, J & Co. (Gale Shipping Co.) 40
Galloway, Col.W. I. 68
Ganges, HMS Appendix H
Gansser, Kapitänleutnant Konrad 20, 26, 75, 78, Note 6, Appendix G
Gavin, Jack Note 9
Gavin, John F. Note 9
General Strike Appendix F
Geneva Convention Appendix C
Germaniawerft (Shipyard) Appendix B
Germany/German(s) 17, 18, 20, 21, 22, 23, 26, 28, 30, 31, 31, 37, 38, 77, 78, Note 6, 14, 21, Appendix C, E
Gerrard, US Ambassador James W. 23, 25, Appendix C
Ghent 23
Gilbert, AB H. Appendix C
Gleaner, HMS 76
Goddard, Paul Appendix A
Goddard, Tessa (née Oxenham) Appendix A
Golberdinge, H. T. H. (sculptor) 32
Goodney, Captain 51
Grand Fleet 18

Great Britain/British 17, 18, 37, 39, Appendix E
Great Central Railway (GCR) 18, 76
Great Eastern Railway (GER) 14, 18, 20, 43, 47, 51, 54, **69**, 77, 78, Note 18, Appendix A, F, H
Great Yarmouth Appendix G
Greenland Appendix G
Greenock Cemetery 76
Grey Collier, Rev. T. 59
Gross Registered Tonnage Appendix I

Hamilton, Lord Claud MP Note 18
Hampshire Chronicle 51
Hannoteau, General 45
Hannover 23, Map C
Harlaam 69
Harte Butler, General Sir Richard 31
Hartnell, First Officer William 23, 25, 27, 44, **67**, Appendix C
Harwich 17, 75, 78, Note 17, Appendix G
  Archives Appendix D
  Corporation Appendix H
  Corporation School 14, **16**
  Further Education Centre Note 3
  General Orders Appendix H
  High School Note 3
  High Steward of Borough of 59
  International Port Map A
  Pepys Street Appendix C
  Town Council 11
  U-boats surrendered at 75, Appendix B
Harwich Railway & Shipping Museum 11
Harwich & Dovercourt Standard Appendix C
Helsinki 76
Henry Robb (shipyard) 40
Hewitt, Geoff 11
Heyst 39
High Seas Fleet Appendix B
Hodder & Stoughton (Publishers) 32, Note 7
Holland/Dutch 18, 30, 77, 78, Note 6
Holy Trinity National School 14
Holzminden 23, Map C

Hook, Ian 11
Hook of Holland 22, Appendix C, Map B
House of Commons 21, 30
Howarth A., Preston Town Clerk 40
Hull 14

Iceland Appendix G
Imperial Merchant Service Guild 3-, 70, Note 18
Imperial War Museum (IWM) 11, Appendix A
Inskip, Suffragan Bishop James 54, Note 19
Inskip, Thomas Walker Hobart Note 19
Ipswich, SS 14
Ireland/Irish 18, Note 13
Irish Republican Army/IRA 68
Ironwood (*Acacia estrophiolata*) Appendix A
Istanbul 75

James Dredging Appendix G
Jarrow Quay 40
John Brown (Shipbuilders) 75
John Bull Ltd. Appendix G
Jutland, Battle of Appendix B, C

Kaiser Wilhem II 28, 30, 44, Note 6, Appendix E
Kent & East Sussex Railway Note 17, Map B
Keyes, Admiral Commanding Dover Patrol Sir Roger 48
Kiel 75, Appendix B, G
King Albert of the Belgians 40, 45, **67**
King Alfred the Great Note 20
King George V 30, Appendix D
King Henry VIII Note 20
King Leopold I Note 8
Köhne, Lutheran Naval Chaplain 27, Appendix C, D
König, Kapitän Appendix G
Kriegsgerichtassessor 25
Kruispoort 27, 72
Krupp Arms Works Appendix B

Index

La Brabançonne (Belgian National
  Anthem) 44
Lady Brussels, SS 41, Note 13
Lady Meath, SS 41, 76, **76**
Last Post 45, Appendix H
Lawrence, Captain F. 51
League of Neutral States (Netherlands
  Section) 32
Le Havre 75
Leicestershire Regiment 44, Note 12
Leipzig Supreme Court Note 6
Leith 40
Leonard, Alan 11
Lichnowsky, German Ambassador Prince 17
Linton (salvage vessel) 38
Liverpool 20, Note 12
Liverpool Scottish (Regiment) 44, 45,
  Note 15
Lloyd Anversois 77
London Midland & Scottish Railway
  (LMS) Appendix F
London & North Eastern Railway
  (LNER) 70, 73, Appendix F
London & North Western Railway
  (LNWR) 32, Appendix F
London 48, 77
  Bishop of 51
  Charing Cross Station 50, 51
  Embankment 50
  GER Memorial 68, **69**
  Liverpool Street Station 32, 33, 51, 68,
    69, Appendix H
  Ludgate Hill 50
  St Pauls Cathedral 50, 51, **52, 53,**
    Appendix C, H
  Tower Bridge Appendix G
  Trafalgar Square 50, Appendix D
  WWII blitz Note 7
Luckett,
  Mrs Dorothy Ada Mary, née Fryatt
    (daughter) 9, 17, 28, Appendix A
  Julian Fryatt (grandson) 11, Appendix A
  Peter Fryatt (grandson) Appendix A
  Simon (great-grandson) Appendix A
Lusitania, SS Appendix G

Maas
  Lightship 20, 22, 25
  River 22, Map B
Malta 76
Mansell, Rear Admiral G.R., CBE, MVO 59
Mantua, HMS Appendix G
March Railway Band 54, Appendix H
Meath, SS (ex-*Lady Meath*) 76
Marinekorps Flandern 27, Note 5
Mauritius 65
Mediterranean 26
Mercantile Marine 48, 54, Appendix D, H
  War Medal Note 8
  Uniform Act 1919 Appendix E
Merchant Navy 48, Note 11
MI6 77
Middlesborough 76
Ministry of Health 62
Mons, Battle of/Retreat from Note 14
Morecambe 18
Mount Fryatt 65
Mulga (*Acacia aneura*) Appendix A
Murder of Captain Fryatt, The (booklet) 32
Murder of Captain Fryatt, The (film) 11,
  35, Appendix A
Mur des Fusilles 65, 72

National Archives, Kew 11
National Film & Sound Archive,
  Canberra Note 9, Appendix A
National Health Service 62
Naumann, Major 25
Nautilus Welfare Fund Note 11
Neville, Augustus Note 9
New London Appendix G
Newmarket, SS 17
New York Times 29
New Zealand 35, 65
Nord II, SS (later *Wrexham*) 76
Norfolk, Virginia Appendix G
Northern Barrage Appendix G
North Sea 18, 75, Note 10, Map B
Norwich, Bishop of 68

Opium Wars 78
Order of Leopold 34, 45, Note 8
  Knights Cross Note 8
Orpheus, HMS 45, 47, 48, **48**, 72, Note 13
Ostend 18, 45, Map B
Ottawa Citizen Note 21
Oxenham, Mrs Mabel Marjorie
  (née Fryatt) Appendix A

Pain, Mr A.C. (GER director) 44
Parkeston Map A
  The Captain Fryatt (Public House)
    Map A
  Fryatt Avenue 62, Map A
  Garland Road 14, 62, Map A
  Marine Superintendent 60
  Quay 17, 77, Appendix C, Map A
  St Pauls Church 60
  Station Appendix H, Map A
Pembrokeshire 20
Plummer, Ray 11
PMV 48, **49**, 50, 132
Police 48, Appendix H
Pollock, Bishop Bertram 68
Port Glasgow 41
Portland stone 54
Portugal (hospital ship) 75
Poulet, Minister of Marine M. 39
Pounds Farm Appendix H, Map A
Premnitz Appendix C, Map C
President de Leeuw (Belgian tug) 40
Preston 40, 41
Preston Guardian 40
Prisoners of War Appendix C
Proctor, Olive Note 9
Provident Clerks' & General Mutual Life
  Assurance Association 30
Psalm 23 Appendix D

Queen Elisabeth of the Belgians 45
Queens Own Cameron Highlanders 44
Queeenstown Road, Southampton Note 2

Railway grouping Appendix F
Ramsgate Appendix G

Red Cross VAD 60
Reynolds, Harrington Note 9
Ribble, River 40
Richardson, Captain C.H., DSC 40
Richter, Matrose 26
River Plate, Battle of Appendix G
Rizeh, Turkey 75
Robertson, Alderman 40
Ronayne, Captain D.I. 40
Rosebank 60
Rotterdam 20, 22, 78, Note 21
Royal Air Force 48
Royal Marine/RM 48, 50, 51
Royal Merchant Seamen's Orphanage 30
Royal Navy/RN 49, 77, Note 10,
  Appendix G
Royal Navy Reserve/RNR 48, 77,
  Appendix J
Royal Navy Volunteer Reserve/RNVR 77,
  Appendix I
Ruhleben (Internment Camp) 23, 24, 28,
  Map C, Appendix C, D
Russia/Russians 75, 76, Appendix C

St Clement, (Admiralty tug) 40
St Dennis, SS 48
Saunders, Harwich Borough Mayor
  Edward 21, 60
Scapa Flow, Orkney 18, Appendix B
Scheld, River 40, 45, Map B
School House, Harwich Note 3
Schouwen Bank 65
Schröder, Admiral Ludwig von 27-29, 44,
  Note 6
Schücking Commission Note 6
Schulte, Kapitänleutnant Appendix B
Scotland 76 Appendix C
Scottish Rifles (Cameronians) Note 14
Scouts/Boy Scouts 44, Appendix H
Second World War 60, 62, 73
Shetland Appendix G
Shields Daily Gazette 40
Shotley Band Appendix H
Sieβ, Kapitänleutnant Gustav 76
Sierra Leone 20

Simon Boliver, SS 60, **62**
Smith & Co., (ship-breakers) 41
South Africa 65
South Eastern & Chatham Railway (SE&CR) 48, Appendix H
Southampton 72, 73
Southampton Daily Echo 72
Southend Appendix G
Spandau 23
Stamfordham, Lord Appendix D
Star, 1914 (Medal) Note 14
Starkey, Second Engineer F.J. 22
Steam locomotives
  Captain Fryatt 32, Appendix F
  Claud Hamilton Note 18
  D14 class Note 18
  D15 Class 51, 54
Stewart, Mrs Dot (great niece) 72
Stiff, Captain 51
Stratford Note 19
  Railway Band 54

Taurus, HMS 48
Teaser, HMS 48
Territorial Force/Army Appendix I
The Hague 77, Map B
The Times 28, 59, 70
Thorp, Rear Admiral Charles F. Appendix H
Thurlow, Chief Engineer F. 22, Appendix C
Tilbury 22, 78, Appendix C, Map B
Tom, British Consul-General Mr Henry 70
Tovill, Chief Steward R.D. 22, Appendix C
Townend, see under *Fryatt*
Townley, Lady Susan 43
Townley, Sir Walter 43
Trafalgar Square 30
Trinity House, Corporation of Note 20
Tulipa 'Captain Fryatt' 69
Tyne, River 49

U-33 (WWI) 26, 75, 78, Appendix E
U-33 (WWII) 76
U-155 Appendix G

U-156 Appendix G
Union Flag 40, 44
Unknown Warrior Note 17

Van Hoestenberghe, Alderman Victor 27, 28
Vellum certificate 21
Versailles, Treaty of Note 6, Appendix B
Victoria Cross Appendix F
Victory Medal Note 8

Wallasey Note 11
Walshe, Percy Note 9
War Crimes Committee Note 6
War Office 51
War Risk 37
West, Andrew 11
Western Front 31
Westminster Abbey Note 17
Wheeler, Cdr G.J. 38
Whitcombe, Suffragan Bishop Robert 54
White, Michael G. 11
Whitwell & Reepham Railway, Norfolk Note 18
Whyatt, AB J.J. Appendix C
Wieder, Leutnant 26
Wilhelmshaven 26
Williams, Major Peter 12
Wilson, Field Marshal Sir Henry MP 68
Winnington-Ingram, Rt, Rev'd. Arthur 51
Wireless telegraphy 20
Worcester, HMS 14
Wrexham, SS 11, 18, **19**, 76, 78

Ymuiden Appendix C

Zapfel, Dr 25, 29
Zeebrugge 23, 37, 38, Note 16, Map B
  Kapitein Fryatt Straat 62
  Mole 23, 37, Note 16
  Raid 38, Note 10
  Tide 38

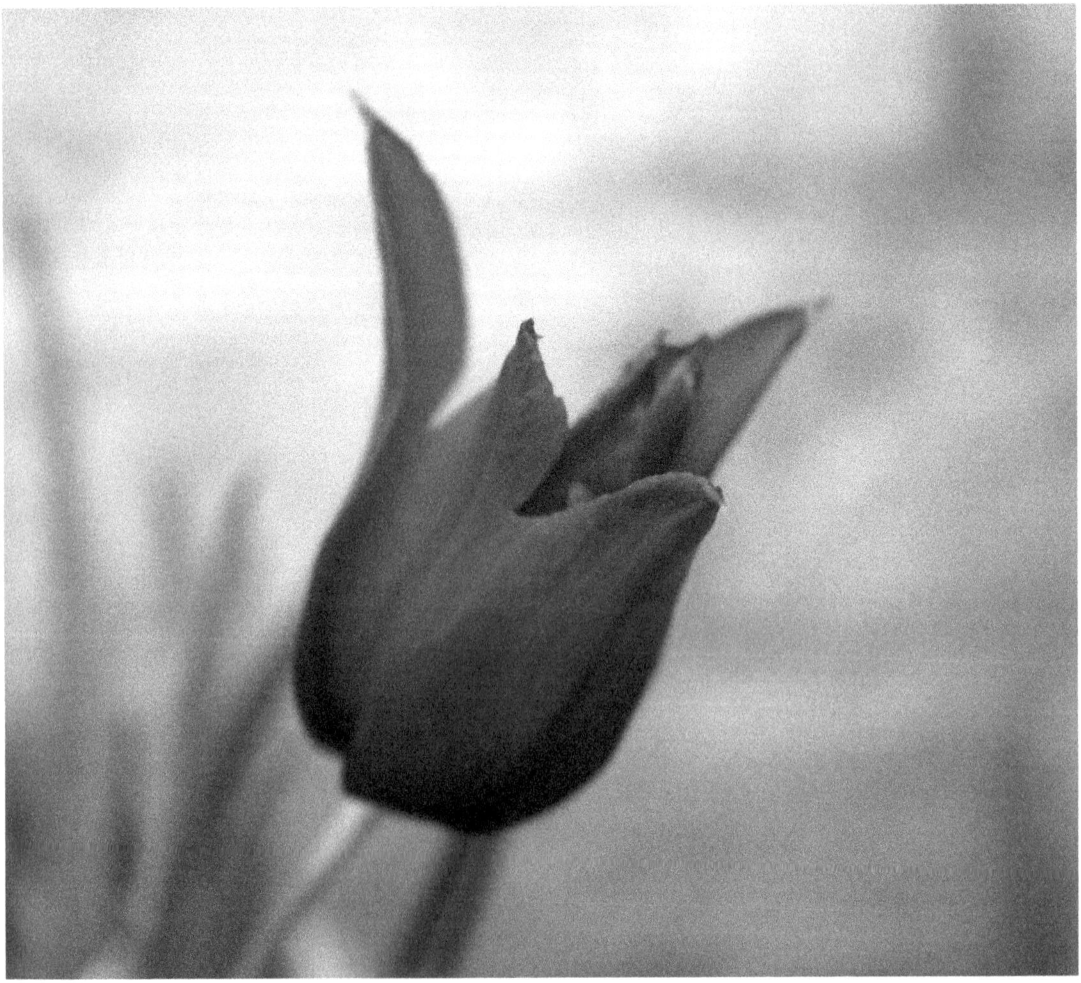

ALSO AVAILABLE FROM AMBERLEY PUBLISHING

Kitchener's New Army: Your Country Needs You!

Edgar Wallace, Campbell McCutcheon

A new postscript tells the story of Kitchener's Army in action.

978 1 4456 2292 7
256 pages, illustrated throughout

Available from all good bookshops or order direct
from our website www.amberley-books.com

ALSO AVAILABLE FROM AMBERLEY PUBLISHING

THE FIRST WORLD WAR IN PHOTOGRAPHS

1914

OVER BY CHRISTMAS

JOHN CHRISTOPHER & CAMPBELL McCUTCHEON

1914: The First World War in Photographs

John Christopher & Campbell McCutcheon

1914: the first year of the 'war to end all wars'. The First World War changed the art of war forever; here the authors document the horrors of war in the photographs of those times.

978 1 4456 2181 4
176 pages, illustrated throughout

Available from all good bookshops or order direct
from our website www.amberley-books.com

ALSO AVAILABLE FROM AMBERLEY PUBLISHING

THE FIRST WORLD WAR IN PHOTOGRAPHS

1915

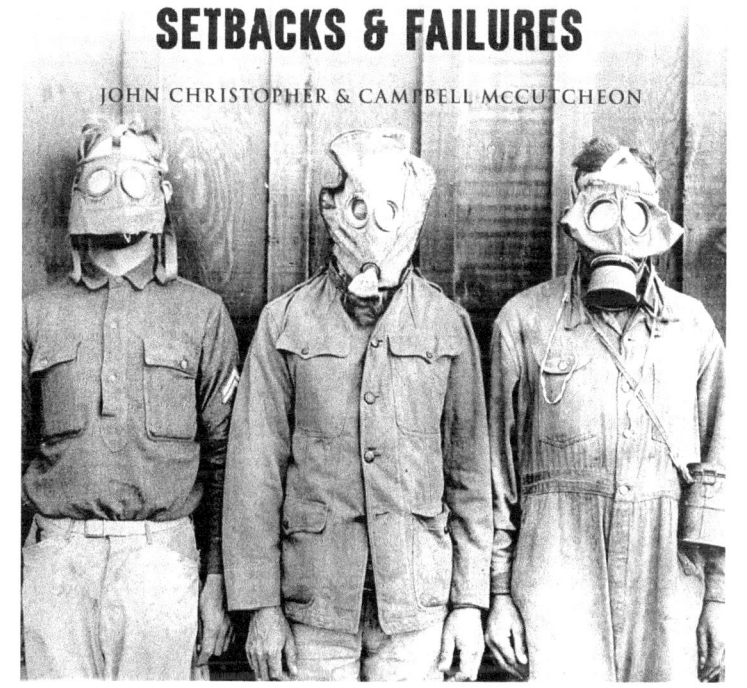

SETBACKS & FAILURES

JOHN CHRISTOPHER & CAMPBELL McCUTCHEON

1915: The First World War in Photographs

John Christopher & Campbell McCutcheon

1915, the second year of the Great War, was to see the failure of the Dardanelles landings and the sinking of the Lusitania. Here, the authors tell the story of 1915 at war using many rare and often unpublished images.

978 1 4456 2205 7
176 pages, illustrated throughout

Available from all good bookshops or order direct from our website www.amberley-books.com

ALSO AVAILABLE FROM AMBERLEY PUBLISHING

THE FIRST WORLD WAR IN PHOTOGRAPHS

1916

A WAR OF ATTRITION

JOHN CHRISTOPHER & CAMPBELL McCUTCHEON

1916: The First World War in Photographs

John Christopher & Campbell McCutcheon

1916, the third year of the Great War, was to see the introduction of conscription for the first time in Britain. Here, the authors tell the story of 1916 at war using many rare and often unpublished images.

978 1 4456 2208 8
176 pages, illustrated throughout

Available from all good bookshops or order direct
from our website www.amberley-books.com

ALSO AVAILABLE FROM AMBERLEY PUBLISHING

THE FIRST WORLD WAR IN PHOTOGRAPHS

1917

MUD AND TANKS

JOHN CHRISTOPHER & CAMPBELL McCUTCHEON

1917: The First World War in Photographs

John Christopher & Campbell McCutcheon

1917, the fourth year of the Great War, saw another year in the trenches for millions of troops mobilised in Europe. Here, the authors tell the story of 1917 at war using many rare and often unpublished images.

978 1 4456 2210 1
176 pages, illustrated throughout

Available from all good bookshops or order direct
from our website www.amberley-books.com

ALSO AVAILABLE FROM AMBERLEY PUBLISHING

THE FIRST WORLD WAR IN PHOTOGRAPHS

1918

END GAME

JOHN CHRISTOPHER & CAMPBELL McCUTCHEON

1918: The First World War in Photographs

John Christopher & Campbell McCutcheon

John Christopher and Campbell McCutcheon tell the story of 1918, the fifth and final year of the Great War, using many rare and often unpublished images.

978 1 4456 2212 5
176 pages, illustrated throughout

Available from all good bookshops or order direct
from our website www.amberley-books.com